Marie S. Miller

History of Flower Arranging ...

OCCIDENTAL FLOWER ARRANGEMENT
600 B.C. — 1900
Traditional Design
Oriental — China — Japan
Occidental
Classical Greece — 600-146 B.C.
Imperial Rome — 28 B.C. — 325 A.D.
Renaissance — 13th-16th Centuries
Dutch-Flemish — 17th-18th Centuries
Early American — 17th Century
French
Baroque — 17th Century
Rococo — 18th Century
Louis XVI & Marie Antoinette — 18th Century
Empire — Napoleon — 19th Century
Colonial Williamsburg — 18th Century
Georgian — English — 18th Century
Early Georgian — Chinese — Italian Influence
Late Georgian — French Rococo Influence
Federal — (George Washington) — 19th Century
Victorian — (Queen Victoria) — English — 19th Century
Early Victorian — French Influence
Mid Victorian
Late Victorian

AMERICAN CONTEMPORARY DESIGN
1900 — 20th Century

Conventional — Geometric Designs
        Line — Oriental Influence
        Mass — Occidental Influence
        Mass-Line — American Origin

CREATIVITY
1960 — Designs for Today and Tomorrow
        FREE FORM
                Naturalistic
        ABSTRACT
                Eclectic Design
                Kinetic Designs
                        Mobiles
                        Stabiles
                Assemblages
                        1. Collage
                        2. Several units within a niche
                        3. One form, free standing sculpture
                Rectilinear Design
                Curvilinear Design
                Constructions
                Psychedelic Design
                Op-Art Designs
                Painting-Arrangements
                Floral Transparencies
                Vibratile Designs
                Aerial Designs — with music effects

New Dimensions In Floral Design

Marie S. Miller, author

PHOTOGRAPHY BY:

Forest Brown

of

Brown's Studio

and

Ward Robertson

All arrangements and paintings by the author

ISBN 0-9606424-0-4 Edition Bind, 3000 copies
ISBN 0-9606424-1-2 Paper Back, 7000 copies

PRINTED IN THE UNITED STATES OF AMERICA

Wegferd Publications
North Bend, OR 97459

and

Times Litho
Forest Grove, OR 97116

Acknowledgements

To My Husband

Wendell W. Miller

For his genuine interest, encouragement, patience and expertise of floral mechanics. Without his help, this book would never have been published.

Our sons, Fritz, Rex and Kirk Miller for their help and interest.

To My Mother

Alice Bettencourt

For the artistic ability she gave me and the inspiration and guidance through the years.

To my two sisters-in-law, Mamie L. Miller and Lillian M. Tyng for baby sitting our three boys so I could attend flower show schools to become a judge and an instructor in floral design, and for their interest and help in so many ways, I am forever grateful.

I am deeply grateful and indebted to my friend and teacher in floral design, Frances Gregg, for her endless help and encouragement through the years, and now my critic and advisor for this book.

To Fern Card, who was my first inspiration in "Grass Roots Gardening" who introduced me to The National Council of State Garden Clubs Inc., and taught me how to exhibit in standard flower shows.

My thanks to Lucile Romig and Phoebe Staples for their judging companionship and advice through the years.

My thanks to all of my garden friends who helped to make this book possible.

Introduction

The purpose of this book is to share with you inspirations of floral design from the beginning of flower arrangement history to creative designs of today.

Although creativity is my main inspiration, I consider it is important to follow the continuity of floral design as it has evolved through a series of changes to the present time.

Using as guidelines, the Handbook for Flower Shows, published by the National Council of State Garden Clubs, Inc., (1977 Edition) the following chapters illustrate and identify the design categories taught in the Flower Show Schools and exhibited in Standard Flower Shows which are sponsored by the National Council of State Garden Clubs Inc. May these examples help the exhibitor, student, judge, instructor and the public to a better understanding and to be able to identify the design categories when they are exhibited in Standard Flower Shows.

Flower arranging has been recognized as a comparable art form to painting, sculpture, music and other fine arts for a number of years. As in the other arts, progress does not stand still. The later chapters in this book serve to illustrate how flower arrangement can be combined with the other arts into one aesthetic unit by the organization of the selected elements according to the principles of design to attain beauty, distinction, expression and harmony in a new approach to floral creativity. May these chapters inspire the arranger to new approaches to floral design.

Table of Contents

Part 1

Introduction to Period Arrangements

It seems the logical approach to defining period arrangements as authentic should be compared to our philosophy on Japanese arrangements. We say "in the Japanese manner" because we do not understand or practice the religious symbols and traditions that have determined their designs. It is nearly impossible to obtain authentic containers used for instance, in the Sung dynasty in China, about the year 960 or even as late as the time of Napoleon, unless one can obtain such items from museums. But for the purpose of flower shows this is quite unlikely or feasible.

We can identify typical shapes of period arrangements, the varieties of flowers used, the types of vase or containers, but it is difficult, if not impossible to be truly authentic in reproducing period designs. In reviewing history, it appears very possible that the arrangements of the Dutch-Flemish Period arose from the paintings of the early Dutch Artists rather than the artists painting from a flower arrangement as their art subject. The abundance of many kinds of flowers during that time were prized for their individual beauty by the painters such as Van Gogh with the sunflowers.

If today we were to compare a mass-line arrangement designed on the West Coast of the United States with the same design made on the East Coast with the same requirements, it is possible there would be quite a variation in the two designs. The influence of the two different regions, the life style of the people, the economy factor of the arranger, climate, and the season in which the design was made, would all have a bearing on the final product.

Flower arrangement today is a rich accumulation of flower arranging history from the past. The inception of the art of flower arrangement dates from ancient Egypt, Greece, India and China.

Therefore, striving to do my best toward authenticity, and my apologies if in error, I present what I think arrangements were like during the period arrangements of the past.

Traditional Design Oriental

I. Chinese Flower Arrangement

History tells us from ancient scrolls, prints, tapestries and porcelains from the 12th to 18th century, during the Sung, Ming and Ch'ing Dynasties that China used cut blossoms of peonies, chrysanthemums, quince, daisies, and many other flowers, branches of flowering fruits and other plant material informally arranged in handsome porcelain vases.

The basic concept of Chinese philosophy is that man is conceived as only one of the purposes of nature, that he is designed to return to the elements. This closeness to nature, along with the influence of Buddhism religion from India in the first centuries after Christ, has become the dominant force in Chinese culture and history.

China has always had a universal love of natural beauty. Emphasis is on naturalism, not stylized design like that of the Japanese. Each composition includes a strong, erect, highly colored and dominant male element, called yang; and the secondary line, a smaller finer delicately tinted and formed horizontal female element, ying which is also expressed in dainty vinelike plant materials. Chinese floral art is less restrained and more colorful; the compositions are cheerful and life-like using objects that are related in line and form. A well executed Chinese arrangement is equivalent to a composition in a painting, with the principles of design carried out to perfection. Balance is of utmost importance. Finer points of line and balance are carried out in plant materials and objects within the design. Beauty of line is emphasized as the first consideration with mass playing a subordinate role. Each Chinese floral design can be reduced to a skeleton of structure. Lines are not static, but are forceful and portray a sense of movement and life. Horizontal lines suggest peace and rest, while curved lines suggest grace and motion.

China has long been recognized as having produced the most beautiful, distinguished vases, many of which are among the most cherished art objects in the world. Vases were intricately decorated with layer upon layer of enamel painted within patterns of brass raised from the brass surface of the vase. Bisque was made during the K'ang period of 1662-1722. China introduced neutral glazes which were ideal for displaying flowers, in harmony with their natural beauty. Vases and dishes were placed on stands, carved teakwood bases or solid bases of porcelain, brass, pottery or wood.

What have we derived from Chinese floral art?

1. The principles of design and importance of balance.
2. Emphasis of line as an essential element with mass being secondary.
3. Natural beauty of each flower casually arranged.
4. Skeletal structure of design.
5. Expression of line — forceful, inspiring, restful.
6. Subdued earthly tones in containers.
7. Our assemblage within a niche in Creative design is a close replica of Chinese floral designs using several related objects with line and forms repeated.

CHINESE ARRANGEMENT

CHINESE COMPOSITION

II. Japanese Flower Arrangement

The introduction of the Buddhist religion in 553 A.D., brought about an awakening of floral art as well as in religion in Japan.

The two founders of floral art in Japan were Prince Shotoku and his cousin, Ono-no-Imoko, they were indirectly responsible for the development of flower arrangement as a distinct art. The two noblemen lived near a lake within the temple grounds and spent much of their leisure time grouping flowers to beautify the altar of the temple, according to the custom of the Chinese, and thus created the first Ikebana or flower arrangement, built around religious symbols and nature. Later the cousin was appointed headmaster of a school that was formed for flower arrangement. The school was called Ikenobo, meaning "the priest by the lake." The art of flower arrangement then spread to the nobility where it was practiced in their homes as well as by the priesthood in the temples. Innumerable schools of flower arrangement developed after Ikenobo.

The influence of simplicity in Japanese arrangement started in the fifteenth century when the Zen tea ceremony came into being. The priests of this religious sect advocated simplicity, austerity, and absence of all elaborate ritual in protest against any luxury, elaborate decor. The special tea room became a meeting place of the people where religious tea ceremonies were held. Unornamented, the walls were paneled in beautiful natural wood, kneeling mats for the tea drinkers and an alcove at one end to hold a wall scroll or painting and a simple flower arrangement. The tea ceremony is still a vital part of Japanese life, with the position for the flower arrangement, the decorative picture or scroll the same as ancient times. The flower arrangement must be placed in such a way as never to hide the wall decoration in any way. During this period, a style of flower arrangement developed known today as "Nageirebana" which is popular throughout Japan. They did not follow the rules exactly of the regular Ikebana, nor did they disregard them entirely.

Another influence of simplicity to Japanese flower arrangement during the 15th Century was introduced by a Japanese by the name of Ashikaga Shogun, Yoshimasa, who was at that time ruler of the country. He introduced simplicity into floral design which was influenced by his love of simplicity in buildings. He built into these first houses what is known as the "tokonoma" a built in alcove intended as a shrine to contain objects of art as well as the flower arrangement. The new simplified form of Japanese flower arrangement was known as "Seikwa."

The fundamental principles of Japanese flower arranging is that the art of arranging is founded on a re-creation of floral growth which includes stems, leaves, flowers and branches, showing the whole character of the plant and achieving dynamic compositions many of which are highly stylized.

Japanese flower arrangement has symbolism in all things. All plant materials, animals, birds, insects, containers, etc. have religious meanings. Seasons of the year are expressed through their floral art. Whatever the style or school, natural growth patterns and blooming period are of utmost importance. Cut flowers and accessory materials are placed as in nature, with buds, blooms and foliage as they are found in growth, though groomed and pruned to sophisticated perfection. Buds of roses, chrysanthemum or iris rise above the other plant material as they are found in nature. Aquatic materials are always placed in low, open dishes with plenty of water visible. Japanese schools often use one plant material alone. When two materials are used, one usually forms the main or heaven line while the other gives secondary and focal interest.

Three main parts or lines are their underlying principles which represent **Heaven** as the highest line, **Man** as the second highest line, and **Earth** the shortest line. When these three principal stems are arranged harmoniously, they will constitute a perfect line arrangement or a foundation for the more elaborate compositions.

Lines have different emotional connotations and vary in their movement and in the forms they create. Vertical lines express strength and character and are bold. Gentle curves have a quality of softness and continuity. Horizontal lines suggest stability, tranquillity and rest. In all Japanese arrangements, the angle of placement is an important factor in achieving correct perspective of design. While each line is different, the visual weights balance each other with emphasis placed on line and form rather than on color. There are no casual lines; materials are placed to support the dominating lines and add grace and form to the arrangement.

All Japanese compositions are three dimensional and have fine qualities of balance and spacing. Lines are vibrant and rhythmic to give an illusion of captured growth. The Japanese have a great sensitivity to nature, arranging water plants in containers such as white, pale green, blue or black to suggest water.

The Japanese prefer to use unadorned and simple containers so as not to detract from the floral design. Accessories are used with restraint and are a symbolic reference when used.

Contrast and asymmetry are fundamental in Japanese flower arrangement and in their homes. Behind the graceful beauty and effortless charm of a Japanese flower arrangement lies the answer — simplicity.

The basic styles of Japanese arrangements are:

Classical: Formal
              Semi-Formal
              Informal

Naturalistic:
              Nageirebana
              Moribana

(See color illustration, page 33)

JAPANESE — SEIKA STYLE
(Classical)

JAPANESE — MORIBANA
(Free Style)
(Shallow container with water)

JAPANESE — NAGEIRE STYLE

(Casual)

What have we learned from Japanese flower arrangement that applies to American design today?

1. Asymmetrical balance.
2. Simplicity and restraint — "understatement" as in abstract design.
3. Depth to floral design through three different heights with triangular dimensions.
4. Plant materials arranged as natural growth.
   a. If grown assymmetrical, it is placed in design assymmetrical.
   b. Stages of bloom as naturally grown, from bud, to full bloom.
   c. Plant material rising from one stalk as their formal styles which we call self-contained balance.
   d. Naturalistic use of accessories vs. decorative.
   e. Water features in American design.
5. Space as a positive factor.
6. Self-expression influenced by symbolism vs. decoration.
7. Use of all parts of plant life; branches, weathered wood as well as flowers.
8. Disciplining materials by gently bending to desired curves.
9. New looks at old materials in recent years (babybreath)
10. Stylized design — found in creative design today.
11. Flower Show Schools have been established, patterned after the Japanese schools teaching discipline in the use of plant materials, containers, simplicity, design elements, principles and attributes and studying the historical background of flower arrangement.

Traditional Design
Occidental

Occidental Flower Arrangement includes all of the European "Period" styles, which were predominantly massed arrangement; Early American and Colonial Williamsburg arrangements strongly resembled the European styles. Arrangements in the Western World have never been a necessary part of religious ceremonies and emphasis has always been on mass and color, with attention mainly to the blossoms, while the Japanese have developed their art to include stems, leaves, flowers, rocks, branches, showing the whole character of the plant, and their arranging is built around a religious philosophy.

The floral art of Europe has been a bouquet art,

History leads us to believe that the first flower arrangement began in ancient Egypt during the years of about 2800 to 28 B.C., with the beginning of floral art used in religious ceremonies, for decorative purposes in the home and for personal adornment in the form of wreaths worn on their heads, garlands, or decorative collars presented to guests. During the reign of Cleopatra, about 30 B.C., flowers were so abundant in Egypt that she used rose petals as carpets in the royal ballroom and on her ships. Flowers were shipped to Rome. Violets, Madonna lilies, narcissus, jasmine, roses, lotus and many other plant materials were used as cut flowers. Fruits, vines and foliage were also used. The refined culture of Egypt and the use of plant materials have been excavated from Egyptian tombs, the most recent that of King "Tut" Tutankhamun, revealing the highly civilized arts of Egypt.

Tracing Occidental Flower Arrangement further in history, we find that in Ancient Greece about 600 to 146 B.C., a floral art existed which was characterized by simplicity and symmetry of form in wreaths, garlands and personal adornment with olive branches and leaves commonly used. There is not proof of cut flowers in vases as in the Egyptian period. Flowers were used in religious ceremonies, and garlands of flowers were used for funerals and to decorate graves. Fruits, flowers and vegetables were combined and presented in baskets at royal banquets and other occasions. Favorite flowers during the Greek period included roses, iris, lilies, hyacinths, narcissus, violets. Olive leaves, grape leaves and laurel leaves were combined with the flowers in garlands and wreaths.

Imperial Rome during 28 B.C. to 325 A.D. was influenced by the customs of Greece using flowers and fruits arranged in low baskets for royal occasions where guests were crowned with massive floral wreaths and garlands. Rome had become very luxurious and the use of plant materials was elaborate and almost overdone. They followed the style of early Egypt in the lavish use of cut roses used as carpets at royal occasions for color and fragrance.

During the Middle Ages about 470 to 1400 A.D. little is known of flower art until the thirteenth century when there is evidence that flowers, fruits and foliages were used at the end of the dark ages of medieval times. This time in history is best remembered for the Gothic period which influenced the use of the Gothic arch in architecture in churches even today.

The highlight in history in flower arrangement came with the Renaissance which was the "rebirth" after the dark ages which began in the fourteenth century in Italy and lasting into the seventeenth century. The Renaissance was a period of vigorous artistic and intellectual activity which gradually moved across Europe. It was a transitional movement between medieval and modern times.

DUTCH AND FLEMISH

(See color illustration, page 33)

The Renaissance Period
13th — 16th Centuries

No doubt flower arrangement was influenced by the other arts. A rebirth in classical forms of art, literature, poetry, sculpture, painting and architecture started in Florence, Italy by the Florentines between the 13th and 16th centuries and flourished until the last works of Michelangeo. Along with the rebirth, intense colors were used in paintings, costumes and wall hangings. White plastered walls brought contrast to the warm colors accented by cool colors. There was a richness in all designs and paintings.

Plant materials used were fresh flowers and flowers dried with their natural colors preserved. Tropical fruits were combined with flowers. Containers were mainly bronze, marble or heavy Venetian glass.

The Dutch Flemish Period
17th and 18th Centuries

Holland had an abundance of flowers during this period. A crowded massing of all available flowers and many varied accessories was typical of this period. Dutch trading ships brought containers from other parts of the world. It was a rich time in arrangement history. Flower arrangements were large with many different kinds of flowers in them. They particularly liked to use tulips, as this was the time that tulips were so popular in Holland when many people lost a fortune growing tulip bulbs when the price went down. Another favorite flower during the Dutch Flemish Period was cabbage roses. Accessories such as bird's nests with eggs, squirrels, rabbits, butterflies and fruits were placed at the base of the arrangement.

Containers were of alabaster, pewter, amber or green glass, silver or other metal in shapes such as ewers, bowls, baskets and others. The arrangements were oval in form and massive.

The French Periods
16th — 17th — 18th Centuries

Early French Period arrangements were of the bouquet form, with little thought given to design. Flowers were light and airy with some color grouping but no center of interest. The French changed their styles of decorating and preference in colors as often as the political situation changed.

BAROQUE PERIOD
1643 — 1715

The Baroque Period started in Italy in the late 16th century and ended at the close of the Renaissance which had spread throughout Europe. Michelangelo is recognized for his extravagant paintings in cathedrals which were characterized by ornate boldness and beauty. Colors were rich and dark, or sometimes subdued with light areas. William Hogarth, English painter, humorist and social satirist introduced the "Hogarth Curve" used in designs today. A graceful "S" curve as the line in an arrangement. Characteristics of the Italian Baroque influence was varied forms of larger flowers at the outer edges, resulting in a vigorous and masculine style, while in France, arrangements were delicate, light and airy with rhythmic motion and the first indication of open areas within the design. Favored colors were: rouge, cream, gold, deep blue and putty. Containers were made of alabaster, crystal, porcelain, Dresden and silver. Shapes of containers were urns, epergnes, compotes, of many sizes, vases, and fruit baskets trimmed with gold.

BAROQUE PERIOD
(See color illustration, page 34)

ROCOCO PERIOD
1715 — 1774

In architecture a name given to the debased style of decoration which succeeded the first revival of Italian architecture. The ornamentation consisted of panels with moldings broken or curved at the angles and filled with rock-work, leafage, shell-work, musical instruments, marks, etc. This style prevailed in Germany and Belgium during the 18th century and in France from the time of Henry IV to the French Revolution. Departing from simplicity, the true principles of decoration were violated, hence the bizarre character of this decoration soon failed to please. Flower arrangements carried the influence of the architecture with the use of shells, scrolls, cupids

ROCCO PERIOD
(See color illustration, page 34)

**Louis XVI and Marie Antoinette
1774 – 1793**

The French flower arrangements of Louis XVI were affected by two schools of thought — the classical and the feminine — represented by delicate, cool colors, highlighted with gold. Marie Antoinette's favorite color was turquoise, though blue, rose, dusty pink, pearl gray and sage green were also widely used. Containers were in the spirit of those used during the reign of Louis XV, with tall slender urns most favored for formal occasions. There was no marked change in kinds of flowers used.

and other feminine characteristics dictated by Madame Pompadour for the French court. Design was asymmetrical. Graceful arcs formed the dominant lines in the arrangement. Flowers were delicate and airy with subtle colors. There was great contrast from the heavy masculine Baroque styles. Favored colors were: apricot, peach, cream, ashes of roses, sage green, beige, turquoise and powder blue. Flowers used were: carnations, daisies, pansies, lilacs, honeysuckle, roses, and many flowering shrubs and vines. Containers were of Dresden china, bisque, alabaster, Venetian glass, silver and bronze found in shapes of compotes, cornucopias, urns, vases, bowls, baskets and epergnes. Delicate accessories are indicated in interpreting the French Rococo influence such as dainty porcelain figurines, lace fans and black eyemasks. Rococo flower arrangement was truly of French origin.

EARLY FRENCH PERIOD
(See color illustration, page 34)

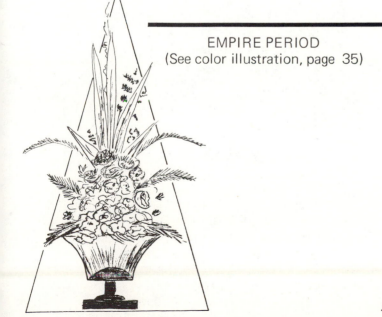

EMPIRE PERIOD
(See color illustration, page 35)

**The Empire Period
1799 – 1815**

Flower arrangements of the Empire Period were more compact than those of earlier French Periods, with simple lines in a triangular design and strong color contrasts.

Napoleon, who dictated the styles of that period, selected red, green, white and gold as his favorite colors. He loved violets which was an Egyptian influence.

The feminine interest was in grayed values of the hues used in previous periods. Yellow, royal purple and bottle green were used with white considered a smart decorative note.

EARLY AMERICAN
1607 – 1720

Colonial Americans placed their flowers and herbs in a mixed bouquet, arranged in whatever utensils were available as they were limited to what they could bring with them to the new world. Household utensils, frequently copper or pewter, pitchers, were used. Also brass, salt glaze, Chinese porcelain, Dutch Delftware and earthenware were used. Arrangements of this period were primitive in style as influenced by the rugged frugal way of life of the early American colonists. There was little evidence of planned design or color grouping in their arrangements. Bright color used with white as a contrast was popular. Plant materials used were common garden flowers such as bachelor buttons, wheat, geranium, grasses, clover, and other wild plants available as they did not have established formal gardens.

EARLY AMERICAN – COLONIAL PERIOD
(See color illustration, page 36)

FEDERAL PERIOD
1780-1830

The Federal Period encompassed the period of history during the time of George Washington's inauguration and the time of Thomas Jefferson, which was Post-Revolutionary. Federal arrangements were of French influence rather than English and were formal mass designs. Color harmony was more important than vivid colors. Height was greater than width. Decorative, formal urns were used with the individual beauty of flowers emphasized. Fruits were combined with flowers and foliages. The flowers were of most common varieties in our gardens today. Blue was a favorite color in various shades, both in flowers and containers. Blue and white wallpaper was formal with disciplined stripes or tiny geometric patterns.

George Washington is credited for the importation of many foreign plants and trees which enhanced the beautiful grounds at Mt. Vernon. Martha Washington is recognized for introducing formal flower arrangement in America.

As "The Father of Our Country" and the great floral contributions they have given us. The Federal Period in arrangement could be emphasized as one of our greater arrangement periods.

FEDERAL PERIOD
(See color illustration, page 36)

COLONIAL WILLIAMSBURG
18th Century

Probably the most elegant of the period arrangements, and the closest to our mass arrangement today, the Colonial Williamsburg period arrangement was often fan shaped, some were rectangular, and others were rather triangular in form. Definite characteristics were: flowers were lightly arranged at the top; those of more solidity were placed close above the rim of the container. Flowers were brought down on both sides of the vase, sometimes completely concealing the container. Accessories of fruit and flowers were usually placed on the table around the container. The height of the arrangement varied from one to four or five times the height of the vase.

In old prints of Colonial Williamsburg designs, flowers used were fresh, with an occasional piece of wheat or barley. There were no dried materials used with the exception of grain stalks.

Containers of the period were vases of classic form, epergnes, pitchers, bowls, cornucopias, in pressed or blown glass, silver, Spode, Staffordshire, Wedgwood, lusterware.

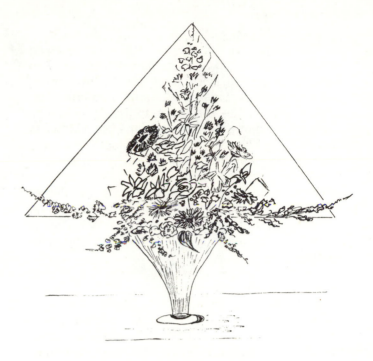

COLONIAL WILLIAMSBURG PERIOD
(See color illustration, page 37)

GEORGIAN PERIODS
1714 — 1820

During the reigns of George I and George II in England, the culture was dignified and imposing.

Early Georgian

Style was influenced by the Chinese and by Italian Baroque, which implied rich, warm colors, and heavy urns of metal or marble.

Late Georgian

Style reflected the influence of the French Rococo in the use of more delicate colors and materials. Containers of porcelain, Delftware, turned wood, were to be found in goblets, baskets, chalices, posey holders, and epergnes.

In both early and later Georgian flower arrangements were symmetrical in form, usually triangular, with the design rich, dignified and elegantly restrained. Textures were velvety, and one kind of flower was often used. All white arrangements were popular, and there was a tendency to use one color with its variations. Could this have been the beginning of our monochromatic color study today?

GEORGIAN PERIOD
(See color illustration, page 37)

VICTORIAN PERIODS
1837 – 1901

The reign of Queen Victoria in England covered a span of sixty-four years — from 1837 to 1901. While court life had always influenced fashions to a considerable extent, perhaps at no time in history has the intimate life of a reigning monarch so dictated fashion in the use of flowers as did that of Queen Victoria. In practically every biographical sketch written about her, mention is made of her love of flowers.

While the general characteristics of flower arrangements were similar throughout the Victorian period, styles were sufficiently different to warrant a division into Early, Mid and Late Victorian.

Early Victorian:

The arrangements of this era reflected a predominant French influence. Textures in containers and figurines were delicate. Although colors were generally rich, pastels were used, and all white was extremely popular.

Mid-Victorian:

All culture in England during this period was influenced by the increasing wealth and power of the middle classes, who showed little restraint or moderation in their arrangements. Flower arrangements suffered by being grossly overdone. The crowding of shorter stemmed flowers into containers brought about the development of the circular form. The width was greater than the height, and height of the plant material less than the height of the container. A massed effect was considered desirable; there was no segregation, dominance or line interest evident; colors were bold and rich, and textures velvety. Often elaborate containers were used. Many kinds of glass, including blown and pressed, milk, hobnail, amber, cranberry and opal were popular. All flowers grown and used in this era are to be seen in American gardens today.

Artificial or dried materials, arrangements under glass domes, Tussie-Mussies and many varied accessories make the true Mid-Victorian arrangement a design we do not find beautiful at present. Modern adaptation of it can be created for use with Victorian furnishings.

Late Victorian:

Flower arrangements of this era became even less artistic, with bouquets more crowded and colors spotted. Grayed values predominated, accented by splashes of vivid color. Containers were heavier and more ornate. Groupings of artificial fruits and flowers made of feathers, sea shells, beads on velvet, were protected under glass domes. This was the period of the "Tussy Mussy" a concentric circle of small flowers arranged around a large central flower. A modified and improved form of the tussy mussy is used today by commercial florists and is called the "Julianne", a rounded form of design using a variety of flowers with babybreath. The height is less than the width of the design. Nosegays are also an outgrowth of the Tussy Mussy.

(See color illustrations, page 38)

SUGGESTED SCALE OF POINTS FOR PERIOD ARRANGEMENTS

	Expressive (with title)	Decorative (without title)
Period Arrangements		
Appropriateness to Period	35	40
Color	20	25
Design	15	20
Distinction	15	15
Expression	15	
	100	100

Conventional Design

1. LINE   **2. MASS**   **3. MASS-LINE**

PART I

Flower arranging is the art of organizing design elements according to the principles of design to attain beauty, harmony, distinction, and expression.

Design principles govern flower arranging as they do all art forms. The difference between flower arranging and the other arts is in the medium.

As gardeners, our medium is plant material.

By predetermining the purpose of the design we are going to create, we have a better idea of the kinds, colors and amount of flowers we are going to need, therefore, we cut fewer plant materials from our gardens.

1. *Occasion of the Design:*
   A *Holiday*
   Consider the colors related to:
   Christmas:
   Red and green, white, silver.
   Easter:
   White, pastel colors. The design may be tall for a feeling of inspiration.
   Birthday:
   Colors would be the favorite of the honoree; interest features such as golf, bird watching, hunting, could be built into a theme.
   Fourth of July:
   Would indicate a patriotic theme with red, white and blue.
   A *Wedding:*
   Depends on the bride's color choice; whether the design is for an altar, the reception table, determines the shape.
2. *In which room is it to be placed?*
   Kitchen:
   One thinks of bright colors for a kitchen. Whether it will be placed on the breakfast table, or a narrow sill, will determine the size and shape of the design.
   Hallway:
   Usually hallways are quite narrow and one passes quickly through a hallway. It is not a room that one spends time in, therefore, bright colors, tall designs, are most appropriate. Or the Zigzag shape we will discuss later in this sec-

tion is appropriate because it is a restless demanding design that one enjoys briefly but would not want to view as one would a design on a dining table.
Dining Table:
A horizontal, restful design in harmony with color of the walls, the draperies, the furniture, and not over 1/3 the width and length of the table. If for dining, the arrangement should be low enough to permit conversation across the table.
Living Room:
Possibly a TV arrangement with consideration of the room appointments, and of where the TV is placed. If it is against a wall, the arrangement can be taller than if it is placed where people pass it when it would be more appropriate to have a lower design.
Coffee Table Arrangements:
The size of the Coffee Table arrangement is determined by the size and shape of the coffee table. Bright color in a low container is most suitable. The design can be tall if there is adequate space in the room to allow comfortable traffic around the table, as in a large hotel lobby. (Or if the design is a coffee table against the wall).
Bedroom Arrangements:
Soft restful colors and textures in harmony with the room appointments are most appropriate.

II. Selection of Plant Materials

Now that we have determined the type of design according to the placement, textures, colors, occasion, and shape, we are ready to select our plant materials.

A. *Flower Forms:*
   a. *Round Forms:*
   All types of round forms, such as daisies, roses, dahlias, carnations, marigolds, petunias.

b. Spike Forms:

Gladiolus, delphinium, iris, snapdragons, stocks, grasses, flowering branches, reeds, pussywillow.

c. Filler Forms:

Babybreath, Statice, forget-me-nots, linaria, any other small dainty flowers that do not detract from the main flower used for a center of interest, that are compatible in color and texture.

(See Plant Conditioning, pages 155 to 166)

III. Conditioning Plant Materials

Conditioning is the first important step towards a fresh distinctive flower arrangement.

1. *Cut preferably in the late afternoon* when the sun has gone down or during the very last hours of daylight, or very early in the morning before the sun is high and the dew has not dried on the blooms and leaves. Plants build up a food supply during the sunny part of the day. At the end of the day, the food content in bloom and stem are at the peak.

2. *Cut with a sharp knife on a slant* of the stem with stems as long as possible. To cut on a slant provides the stem better water intake. A slanting stem cannot rest flat on the bottom of a container to possibly be cut off from the water supply. If one must split harder stems, slanted cut stems are easier to work with than straight cut stems. All soft stems must be cut with a knife. Use sharp pruning shears, or a small saw for heavy branches.

3. *Carry water to garden* and place cut stems in water immediately to avoid air to the stems. Recut stems under water and condition in the same water in which they were cut to prevent air bubbles in new water from the faucet. Soft stemmed flowers which benefit from being recut under water are Carnations, Marigolds, Marguerites, Asters, Sweet Peas, Gladiolus and Chrysanthemums.

4. *Place bucket of flowers in water* in cool dark place out of drafts, as drafts are as hard on flowers as bright sunlight. Avoid a close atmosphere.

(See Types of Plant Material, pages 153 to 154)

Conventional Design

Using the examples of the best work from the Old European Masters and the Classical style of the Japanese, American Contemporary flower arrangement has merged into the mass-line arrangement so commonly found in American homes today.

Conventional designs are organized according to rules, styles or previously executed ideas or patterns. They are based on geometric forms such as the cube, circle, pyramid, crescent, Hogarth Curve, and a number of other geometric forms. These designs have one center of interest near the center axis where all lines converge, but no crossed lines are evident.

All conventional designs must have depth and finished on the back, whether to be viewed from front or both sides.

Conventional designs are planned for decorative purposes in the home rather than expressive communication to the viewer. Designs are enjoyed for their color harmony, textures and fragrance. Graceful rhythm created by gradation of line, texture, color and flower form is characteristic of Conventional designs.

1. *LINE DESIGN* is of Oriental influence. Simplicity is achieved by the restraint in materials used. Line designs are simple and clean cut, resulting in a sharp silhouette of graceful rhythmic line. Flowers placed at a central axis but following the contour of the line are enhanced by the spacious open pattern supported by the linear materials used. Likeness of line direction and materials used are preferred to contrasts. Inspired by natural forms, they depend upon normal patterns of plant growth and existing curves. Flowers and foliages are pruned to clarify line and emphasize simplicity.

2. *MASS DESIGN* is characterized by a closed silhouette with no evidence of a linear pattern. Plant materials and colors are grouped to create pattern. The mass design can be round, oval, triangular or fan shaped. Flowers should never be crowded but can be compact or arranged in an open light airy bouquet such as during the French eighteenth century styles of the reign of King Louis XVI and Marie Antoinette. A center of interest is established at the central axis, using bolder flower forms and brighter hues to add and hold interest. Lighter values of plant materials are placed at the outer edges and top of the design for visual balance. Filler materials such as babybreath add airyness and life to the mass design. Because of the wealth of plant material used in a mass design, it adds a note of elegance and enhances the location, complementing the style and tone of the appointments and is very adaptable and lovely in our homes today.

3. *MASS-LINE DESIGN* is an American origination and is probably the most popular and adaptable design for modern homes today. A Mass-Line design is recognized as having an open silhouette, a pleasing outline and organized placement of materials resulting in a predetermined form. A Mass-Line design can vary between a Line design and a Mass design in the amount of plant materials used but is probably closer to being Mass than Line design. However, the design must possess the linear qualities of Line design through continuity of gradation and transition of materials resulting in a gradual change and creating smooth graceful rhythm. The strongest and greatest depth of the design is at the center axis where all lines converge. Plant materials are of similar nature with combinations featuring related lines, colors, textures and forms with enough contrast to eliminate monotony. The center of interest should be in proportion to the over-all design using bright colors to hold interest.

THREE BASIC FORMS IN RELATION TO SHAPE

1. Sphere

2. Cube

3. Pyramid

(See color illustrations, pages 39-40)

(See color illustrations, page 38 and 39)

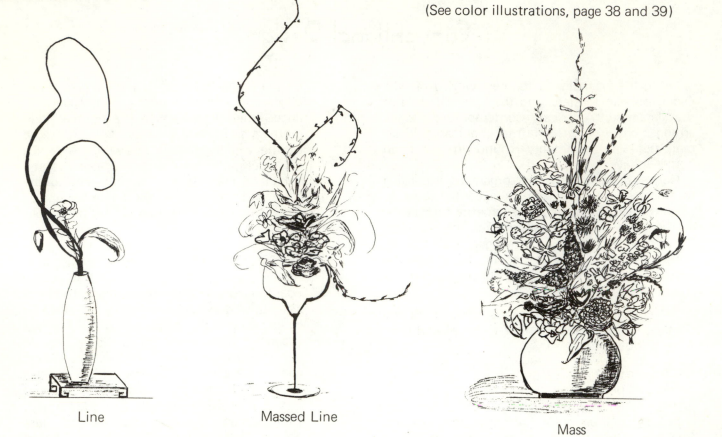

Line

Massed Line

Mass

THREE MAIN TYPES OF DESIGNS
Example: (The Crescent in all three types)

A. Line

B. Massed Line

C. Mass

DEFINITION OF FLOWER ARRANGEMENT:
"Flower Arrangement is the art of organizing the Elements used according to the Principles of design to obtain beauty, distinction, expression and harmony."

SUGGESTED SCALE OF POINTS FOR CONVENTIONAL DESIGNS

Classes specifying type of Design, Color Harmony, Suitability to Placement, or Occasion.	Expressive (with title)	Decorative (without title)
Conformance	10	15
Design	35	40
Color Harmony	20	25
Distinction	15	20
Expression	20	
	100	100

An arrangement in the **"Japanese Manner"**. *Bamboo, large red dahlias and blue spruce branch complete this design arranged on a pagoda shaped sheet of glass. This is but one of many Japanese styles today and the arranger does not attempt to carry out any of the Japanese symbolism used in authentic Japanese arrangements.*

Typical of the **Dutch-Flemish** *period arrangements was the over-abundance of flowers. Flowers were informally crowded in the vase with openness at the top. Arrangements were oval in form and massive. Butterflies, birds, bird nests with eggs, rabbits and other accessories were placed beside the arrangement. It was a rich period in history of floral design.*

Baroque *period arrangements were symmetrical in design with varied forms of larger flowers at the outer edges.*
Favored colors were rouge, cream, gold, deep blue and putty. Some were a vigorous masculine style. Flowers of the day are shown in porcelain urn with rose taffeta background.
1643-1715 — about 72 years.

The **Rococo** *style is truly French in origin. Court styles of the day were dictated by Madame Pompadour. Flowers were delicate and airy, with subtle colors.*
Arrangements were symmetrical.
Flowers in delicate colors and airiness are shown in a formal container with doves on the container.
This style prevailed (in Germany and Belgium during the 18th century), in France to the time of the French Revolution.
1715-1774 — 59 years.

The **French** *flower arrangements of Louis XVI were affected by two schools of thought, the Classical and the Feminine.*
The above French period arrangement depicts the style chosen by Marie Antoinette. Although her favorite color was turquoise, flowers favored delicate colors highlighted with gold.
1774-1793

HISTORY OF NAPOLEON

Napoleon created a nobility with imposing titles; surrounded himself by a brilliant court, in command of 680,000 men. His empire extended from the frontier of Denmark to Naples, including Paris, Rome and Amsterdam, divided into 130 provinces having a total population of 42,000,000. He also had control in confederation of the Rhine. He was a descendant of the Florentines. He was elected the Emperor of France and crowned King of Italy. To have such power — yet he loved flowers!

French Empire Period *arrangements were more compact with simple lines in a triangular design with strong color contrasts. Napoleon, who dictated the styles, selected red, green, white and gold as his favorite colors. The urn with columnar base was the most favored style of container.*
1799-1815

Early American Colonial Period *arrangements were mixed bouquets with bright contrasting colors rather than harmonizing colors.*
Containers were often kitchen utensils and represented the colonial life of early America, showing little refinement in appointments, flowers and containers.
1607-1720

Federal Period *arrangements were mass design with formal balance and French influence.*
Vases of classic form predominated with individual beauty of flowers stressed.
George Washington was responsible for the importation of many foreign plants, trees and shrubs to America.
Martha Washington is credited with introducing formal flower arrangement in America. Arrangements were known for color harmony rather than vivid contrast.
1780-1830

Colonial Williamsburg Period *arrangements were fan-shaped, rectangular or triangular.*
Flowers were lightly arranged at the top with more solid forms above the rim of the container. Flowers were brought down on both sides of the vase. Height of the arrangement varied from one to four or five times the height of the container.
This could have been the beginning of our mass-line designs today.
1720-1780

The **Georgian Period** *covered a span of about 116 years in England during the reign of King George I, II and III. In both early and the later Georgian flower arrangements, symmetrical forms, usually triangular with rich dignified designs, were displayed showing restraint.*
Warm color, often one kind of flower, was used in one color. Possibly a forerunner of our Monochromatic color study today.
1714-1820

The early **Victorian Period** *reflected a predominant French influence. Richly colored flowers of many varieties were used with contrast rather than harmony.*
Arrangements were massed and crowded so much that the individual beauty of flowers was lost.
Arrangements were globular or circular in form. See detail of Mid-Victorian and Late Victorian periods for the change in arrangements during the reign of Queen Victoria.

1830-1901
Reign of Queen Victoria — a period of 64 years.

"Grandmothers Bouquet" — *Common garden flowers of pastel hues were loosely arranged in crystal containers with more width than height. The designs were symmetrical but casual with little thought given to the grouping of colors. Sweet peas, babybreath, roses, gladiolus, Cosmos and Sweet William were among the favorite flowers used.*
A crocheted doily or cutwork linen was popular under the vase.
1890-1940

The 20th Century American Period Arrangement *carries the influence of Colonial Williamsburg in height, elegance, materials brought down over sides of the container as were the Dutch and Georgian Periods.*
The American influence also has patterns of open areas in the top of the design and has a center of interest above the center axis.
A contrast of many bright garden flowers is shown in the above American Mass Design.

*A **True Line** design with graceful clean silhouette of black huckleberry branches with dahlias. The slender black container adds just enough visual weight to give good proportion to the design.*

*A **Round Mass** arrangement with vibrant values of red highlighted by single yellow dahlias and a contrasting outline of dainty babybreath. American mass today is often more bold in color, use of one color and can be geometric shapes other than rounds, ovals or fan shaped as found in the period arrangements.*

FALL GLORY
*A tall **vertical mass-line** design of Pampas grass, red dahlias, feverfew, maple leaves and white gladioli gives an example of a combination of mass and mass-line design. It does not have a closed silhouette as a mass design but also uses more plant material than is usually shown in a true mass-line design. It is shown to illustrate the degrees of variation in the types of designs.*

A naturalistic **mass-line** *with orange dahlias giving gradation to the tall Scotch broom.*
Hosta leaves and a rock covered with barnacles complete the design.

A heavy **mass-line** *design using fasciated mullen, flax pods, orange cactus dahlias, bachelor buttons and hydranga in a heavy pottery container repeating the blue and brown in the plant materials. The shadow on the background helps to visually balance the heavy plant materials.*

Part 2

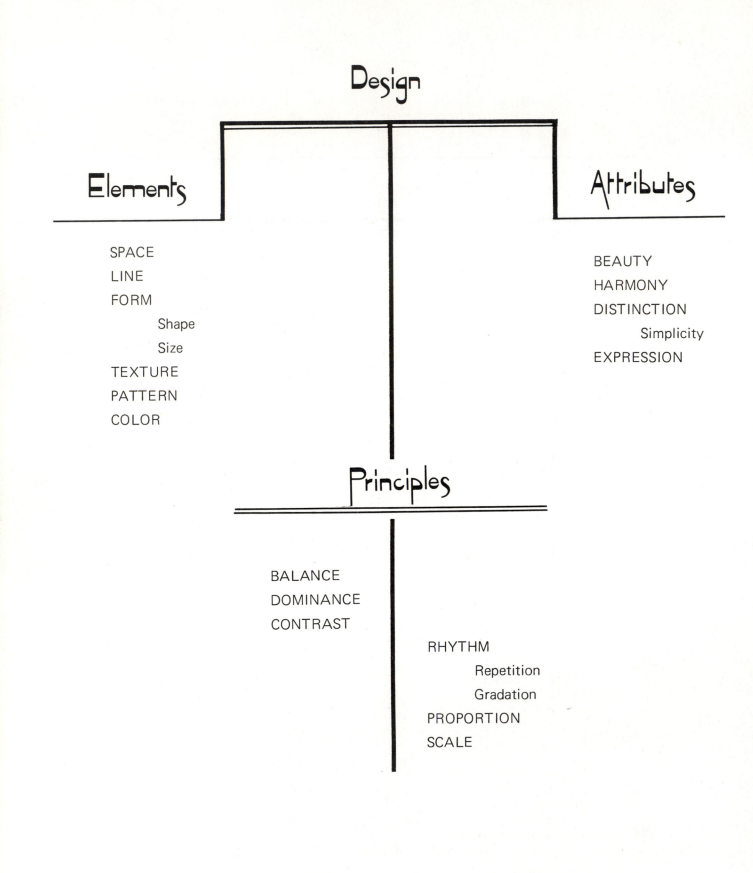

Design

Elements

SPACE
LINE
FORM
      Shape
      Size
TEXTURE
PATTERN
COLOR

Attributes

BEAUTY
HARMONY
DISTINCTION
      Simplicity
EXPRESSION

Principles

BALANCE
DOMINANCE
CONTRAST

RHYTHM
      Repetition
      Gradation
PROPORTION
SCALE

The Elements of Design

I. The Elements of Design

Design elements are the visual characteristics of the physical components. Design elements are the ingredients with which we work. They are as much a part of our everyday living as the sun, the rain, earth, rocks and our rivers.

The elements of design are space, line, form, color, texture, and pattern which must be combined and organized to form a complete unit.

A. SPACE

The arranger works with three kinds of space:

1. The total space, which is three dimensional.
2. Spaces within plant material and other components.
3. Spaces established within the design.

1. The *total space* is that space available to the arranger. In the Flower Show it is determined by the schedule and set up by the staging committee. In the home it is controlled by the surrounding wall area and the furniture. Total space is three dimensional, which includes the height, the width and the depth.

2. *Spaces within plant material* and within other components may be large or small, depending on size and placement of petals, leaves, and branches. In containers spaces may be enclosed by handles or raised bases.
   a. Look at space fluidly within the design and its surroundings.
   b. Space and space relations are our most important factors in design.
   c. Time and space are concerning factors today.
   d. Space can be adjusted.
   e. Space has color and texture through its background.
   f. Space is not like plant material as it is an intangible element.
   g. Space as a positive element has more flexibility than form.
   h. The attributes of space are:
      1. size
      2. shape
      3. position

3. The space established within the design is the element over which the designer has **complete** control. The spaces in the design must be planned and organized by the arranger. It is the placement of lines and forms that determine the size and limits of spaces. A sharp clean silhouette is achieved by trimming out unnecessary plant materials to create interesting spaces. Positive space is the plant material; negative space is the open or closed areas which include color and textures of background for the design.

B. LINE

Line is the primary foundation of design. It is the first of the positive elements to be considered in plan and execution of design. The direction or attitudes of line are:

1. Vertical
2. Horizontal
3. Diagonal
4. Oblique

Characteristics of Line are:

1. Long or short
2. Straight or curved
3. Weak or strong
4. Thick or thin
5. Bold or delicate

Line creates a visual pathway which enables the eye to travel easily through the design. Line serves as the skeleton or structural framework to support the design. Line is a communicating factor, in that it promotes harmony, unity or contrast; and suggests motion.

SHAPE

Shape is not considered to be one of the elements of design according to the Hand Book for Flower Shows by the National Council of State Garden Clubs.

It is a two dimensional form of height and width and the result of converging lines. We have design shapes as they are illustrated in two dimensional form in the following pages. The arrangement takes on FORM when the third dimension of depth is added by means of plant material.

C. FORM

Form is the total effect of the structure of an artistic design. It is above and beyond simple shape or outline in that it is three dimensional. Form may Be:

a. *Closed* — which is solid, compact, as a mass arrangement with few open spaces, or as an individual flower such as a peony or double poppy.

b. *Open* — is illustrated in a Line or Mass-Line design. A Lily or Orchid is considered open form as an individual flower. Spaces are important in creating a design with open form. Irregular form is more interesting to the observer as one cannot see the entire form at a glance but appreciates it for its intricate structure.

Depth of form may be achieved by placing some materials in profile rather than using flat surfaces and by overlapping forms.

D. TEXTURE

The element, texture refers to the surface finish of materials which appeals to sight and touch. It is the character of the surface generally referred to as rough or smooth, coarse or fine, glossy or dull, hard or soft.

For textural harmony, consideration should be given to all components including: background, plant materials, container and accessories.

Texture influences weight. Rough, coarse or dull textures appear heavier. Texture modifies color. Rough, coarse or dull textures tend to reduce value and chroma. Smooth fine textures tend to increase value and chroma.

Textures may be used to add interest to an arrangement. The artist is always searching for new textural relationships as a means of creativity. Texture also adds interest to flower arrangement by contrast in textures. Too much contrast in texture can cause confusion and give the arrangement a weak appearance as too much contrast breaks the unity of the design.

E. PATTERN

Pattern is composed of lines, shapes, forms as well as the spaces between them. Hues, values and chromas form the color pattern. Plant materials such as tulips, florets of gladiolus, have pre-designed pattern, also foliages such as Fatsia, palm leaves, and many others.

The predesigned patterns of the components are used as units in the design. Together the plant material, container and other components form the pattern or silhouette of the finished design.

SIZE

Size does not need to be defined but understanding of its visual effect is necessary. In design the conern is not with actual dimension but with apparent or visual size. Visual size varies with the distance from the viewer, the size of the other components, or things seen at the same time, the color, texture and pattern in the same component.

A flower that might be appropriate in size in an arrangement on a tray would be too small in a larger arrangement. Shiny textures appear to be larger than those with a dull surface.

F. COLOR

Since color is a more complex design element than the ones just mentioned, a chapter has been written on color and the many color harmonies possible in flower arranging.

The art of using color in flower arrangement lies in the practical knowledge and understanding of the color sense itself, the way in which the human eye, brain, and psyche react to what is seen.

Principles of Design

A principle is a fundamental truth which gives special quality or effect. Design principles are basic art standards based on natural laws. Design principles apply to all forms of art including flower arranging, and are the same for all design. The principles of design are: Balance, dominance, proportion, scale, rhythm and contrast.

A. Balance —

Balance is visual stability and equilibrium. It is the result of placing equal weight on opposite sides of an imaginary central axis. The axis is always vertical because balance is related to the force of gravity. Balance should be evident when viewed from all sides.

(1) *Symmetrical Balance* is achieved by identical placements on either side of the central axis. It expresses formality, repose, dignity and stability. Symmetrical balance is equal balance of weight, actual or visual.

(2) *Asymmetrical Balance* is achieved by an off-center placement or unlike units having equal attraction. Visual weight may differ from actual weight. Asymmetrical balance has greater aesthetic appeal than symmetrical balance. There is no rule for achieving this balance.

(3) *Dynamic Balance* is a balance of forces, appearing to have the most motion, creates tension and counterbalance; usually expressed in contemporary or abstract design classes.

(4) *Self-Contained Balance* is achieved within the design itself; it is not influenced by any outside factors. It may be either symmetrical or asymmetrical.

(5) *Balance by Placement* is achieved by having the short side of the area and the short side of the design correspond. The greater the weight of plant material and the general flow of linear interest should be on the same side as the greater area of the base or setting. Example: an off-center placement of the design on a piece of furniture or base that will offset the weight within the design itself.

(6) *Fixed Perspective* — when a center of interest is used where all lines converge, it becomes a fixed perspective. The Geometric designs which will follow, also the Conventional designs of Line, Mass and Mass-Line, have a fixed perspective at the center axis.

(7) *Counter Balance* — is needed when plant material extends beyond the point of support. In order to maintain equilibrium, it must be balanced with an equal force in the opposite direction.

(8) *Static Balance* — is an unmoving balance; so obviously at rest, it does not hold the viewers attention long. It contains an equal distribution of material, physically and visually throughout the design.

Although there is no rule of achieving balance, the following serves as a guide to balance. Denser and bolder forms, larger sizes, darker colors, unusual forms and coarse textures appear heavier. Plant materials placed higher in the design or farther away from the central axis appear heavier than those nearer the center. A reverse of this rule would be a large pastel peony placed at the center axis with a dark value of dainty flowers in the top of the design.

B. *Dominance* — The use of more of one thing than another, giving emphasis and providing dominance.

Dominance is achieved by repetition (grouping of elements) repetition of shape, hue, line or direction, a texture or one idea throughout the design. Too much dominance or lack of subordination leads to monotony with no variety or relief.

C. *Contrast* — is difference. Contrast is achieved by placing opposite or unlike elements together in such a way as to emphasize difference. Contrast exists only between elements that are related in some manner, such as light and dark, smooth and rough, hot and cold. Too much contrast results in confusion, not enough contrast results in monotony. Contrast is necessary to add spice and life to a design.

D. *Rhythm* — is a dominant visual path or direction through the design. There are many variations of rhythm. It may be a smooth rhythm such as a waltz, it could be a short jerky rhythm such as a tango, or it could be a very formal rhythm such as a march, which would be the least exciting in floral design. Rhythm may be achieved by the use of repetition or gradation in a linear direction.

(1) *Repetition* — is achieved by repeating a shape, hue, value, direction etc. Contrast can add life and excitement to a design. Exact repetition becomes monotonous and stops rhythm.

(2) *Gradation* — implies gradual change in size from large to small, in weight from heavy to light, in texture, from coarse to fine, in color, from dark to light, dull to bright, hue to hue and value to value. Repetition and gradation play a subtle but very important supporting part to achieve rhythm.

E. *Proportion*

Proportion is the relationship of areas and amount to each other and to the whole.

In regard to *Line* — it is relative length.

In regard to *form* or *space* — it is relative area or volume.

In regard to *color* — it is relative magnitude, the combined effect of *hue, value, intensity,* and *texture.*

Things are only too big, too much or too little in relation to something else in the design when considering proportion.

F. *Scale*

Scale is size relationship. It is closely related to proportion. Repetition and variation of size are always in good scale. Contrast of size may also be in good scale. It is only when contrast of size is too great that components are out of scale. An extreme example of this was observed in a flower show some years ago, where the exhibitor had two tiny figures standing under a tree with a regular sized bird's nest with a bird of equal size, placed above the couple. One easy way to remember the difference between proportion and scale is this:

Proportion — is like a crowd of people — an amount

Scale — is like a man with his small son — comparison one to one.

The Attributes of Design

Flower arranging is the art of organizing design Elements according to the Principles of design to attain the Attributes which are *Beauty, Harmony, Distinction,* and *Expression.*

We think of the Elements as the tools with which we work. The Principles are the laws of the universe, and the Attributes are the — final product — the reward for our efforts.

Beauty —
is that intangible quality which evokes aesthetic pleasure and delight. All flower arrangements, no matter what category they may be exhibited in, must show beauty to the viewer, or the exhibitor has defeated the purpose intended for flower shows.

Harmony —
is the pleasing arrangement of design elements according to the principles into a unified art form.

Distinction —
is marked superiority in every respect. First, the condition and quality of the plant material and all other parts of the design; the superior quality of design with recognition of originality and creativity; simplicity of design with nothing unnecessary added, nor anything necessary left out.

Expression —
is the quality which communicates to the observer an idea, emotion, mood or story. Arrangement classes with titles emphasizing expression add interest to the show.

Geometric Design

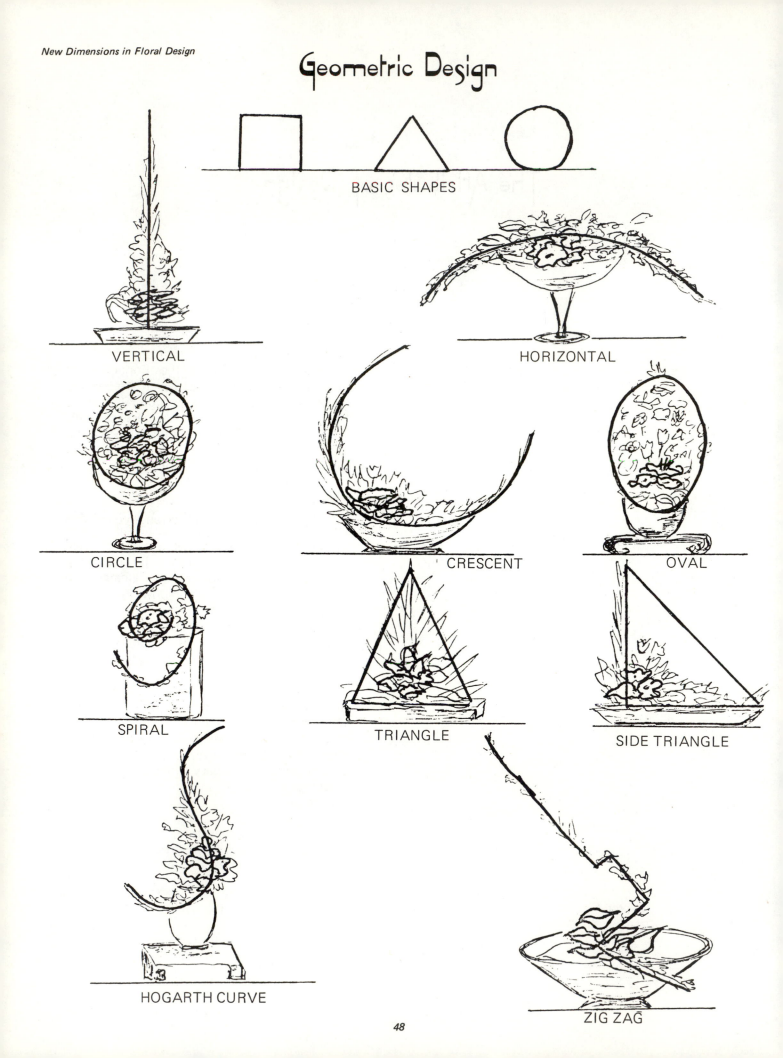

BASIC SHAPES

VERTICAL

HORIZONTAL

CIRCLE

CRESCENT

OVAL

SPIRAL

TRIANGLE

SIDE TRIANGLE

HOGARTH CURVE

ZIG ZAG

Geometric Designs

All geometric designs are based upon the cube, the sphere, and the pyramid. All geometric designs have a center of interest which is located at the center axis.

1. First, line is established
2. Shape is the result of converging lines
3. Form is created by adding depth to shape.

It is important to learn to make flower arrangements of the basic geometric shapes by practice in order to learn to exercise the principles of design from a predetermined design form. Like the piano student who must achieve dexterity and strength in his fingers, the arranger must learn the visual and physical dexterity of flower arranging through practice.

Briefly reviewing history, first were the Oriental and Occidental arrangements which were Chinese, Japanese from the Orient and "Period Arrangements" from the Western World. After the colonies settled in America, along with the Early American arrangements of the settlers which were quite crude, followed a time of the old fashioned "grandmothers bouquet" up until during the 1930's approximately. During these years there was a gradual awakening of garden clubs throughout America and an interest in flower arrangements with a specific design. The basic shapes of the geometric designs illustrated here were popular at that time. Containers in many shapes, colors, textures and sizes became the "in thing" among the garden club arrangers. Geometric designs are still popular.

These basic geometric designs are the basis of all creative combinations in design today. The cube, the sphere and the triangle are as ever present as the elements and principles in all floral design today.

It is important to achieve good design through these geometric designs as a guide to perfection before one attempts creative and abstract design. The old saying, "A house is only as strong as its foundation", is as true with flower arranging. One must have good mechanics, recognize good balance, and how to achieve it, thoroughly understand all of the other principles; how to apply the elements to achieve good design. Old Chinese proverb: "Don't try to catch two frogs with one hand." — Understand the basics.

GEOMETRIC ARRANGEMENTS

1. Vertical
Vertical designs are suitable for hallways as they can be tall and narrow. A round, square or oblong container is appropriate. A vertical design is more effective in a mass-line design or line rather than a mass design. They are very effective as altar arrangements, hall arrangements and entryways. They can be viewed from one side or both sides depending on placement.

2. Horizontal
Horizontal designs are excellent for tea table arrangements, wedding receptions, buffets. This design would be best arranged in a round or oval container and viewed from both sides. Arranging to be viewed from both sides gives added depth to a design. Also best as mass-line.

3. Circle
A round mass design to be viewed from both sides is suitable for table, buffet or TV.

4. Crescent
The crescent shape is an exciting design for beginners and is quite versatile in that it works well as a mass-line design and can be arranged as a line design as well. Gradation is very essential to a crescent design, with the heavier plant material near the center axis and graduated out to slim tips of the crescent. A round container is more harmonious for a crescent than a square container. However, a long narrow rectangular container is very suitable. If designed for a line arrangement, the design has more distinction if the design is raised on a pedestal or slim footed container. The crescent is truly an American creation.

5. Oval

The oval shape serves best as a mass design and is the form of many of the period arrangements in the Occidental tradition. It is a graceful closed form with very small open spaces and silhouette only at the outer edges of the design. It is suitable for the home, church and weddings.

6. Spiral

The spiral shape is one we do not see as often as others. It contradicts the suggestion that round shapes do not look well in square containers. In this case, the contrast of a square pillow container with the rounded line, gives contrast and relief. Trailing Ivy or other soft vines serve well to carry out the line in the design.

7. Triangle

The triangle is an easy one for beginning arrangers to try because it is symmetrical and the shape is easy to follow. The triangle falls in the category of a heavy mass-line with regulated silhouette at the outer edges and top of the design. Suitable for many occasions.

8. Side Triangle

The side triangle is another easy one for beginning arrangers. An oblong rectangle serves well for a container for this design. Ideal plant material to establish the shape of the design is Gladiolus as they can be graduated between the height and the length to achieve dimension and give a refreshing design by adding green plant materials with the Gladiolus. The center of interest in a side triangle, depending on if it is a right handed side triangle or a left sided triangle, will be at the base of the heaviest amount of material at either right or left hand side of the container. The side triangle is often seen in flower shows, and very versatile for the home and many other occasions, as a mass-line design.

9. Hogarth Curve

Possibly the most graceful of all geometric design, it is not one of the easier ones to make but exciting to create a linear pathway throughout the design from top to bottom. One can create a line, mass-line and quite full mass design with the Hogarth shape. It is important always to finish the back of the design for depth even though it is intended to be viewed from one side. Depth adds elegance to mass designs.

10. Zig Zag

The Zig Zag shape is an exhibition "Show off" because it is a very attention getting design. The design is striking and restless, therefore suitable for exhibition purposes, or placed in the home where it will be viewed briefly, as in a wide hallway as one passes through. Depending on the size of the Zig Zag, a large round footed bowl or one with bases under the container relieves the visual weight, especially if the container is a dark value. Serves best as a mass-line design. It could be a line design.

Four Easy Steps to Geometric Designs

1. Vertical	6. Spiral
2. Horizontal	7. Triangle
3. Circle	8. Side Triangle
4. Crescent	9. Hogarth Curve
5. Oval	10. Zig Zag

Step 1. Establishes line.

Step 2. Strengthens line and adds fullness to form

Step 3. Adds visual weight at base of design and covers needle frog and front edge of the container.

Step 4. Places the center of interest at the axis.

Vertical Design

Step 1.　　　　Step 2.　　　　Step 3.　　　　Step 4.

(See color illustration, page 57)

Horizontal Design

Step 1.　　　　　　　　　Step 2.

Step 3.　　　　　　　　　Step 4.

(See color illustration, page 58)

Circle Design (See color illustration, page 59)

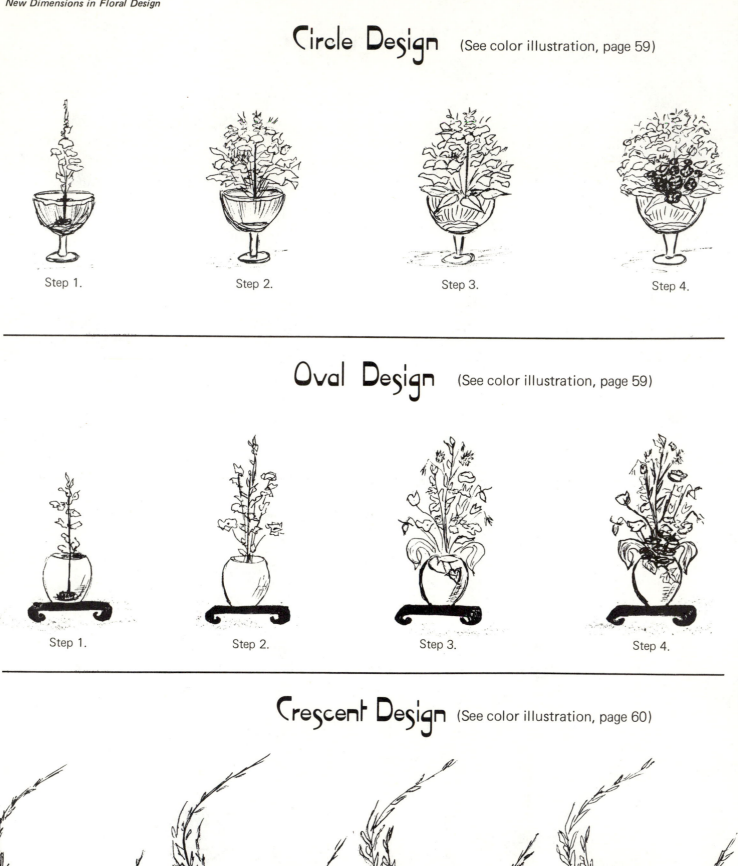

Step 1.   Step 2.   Step 3.   Step 4.

Oval Design (See color illustration, page 59)

Step 1.   Step 2.   Step 3.   Step 4.

Crescent Design (See color illustration, page 60)

Step 1.   Step 2.   Step 3.   Step 4.

Spiral Design (See color illustration, page 60)

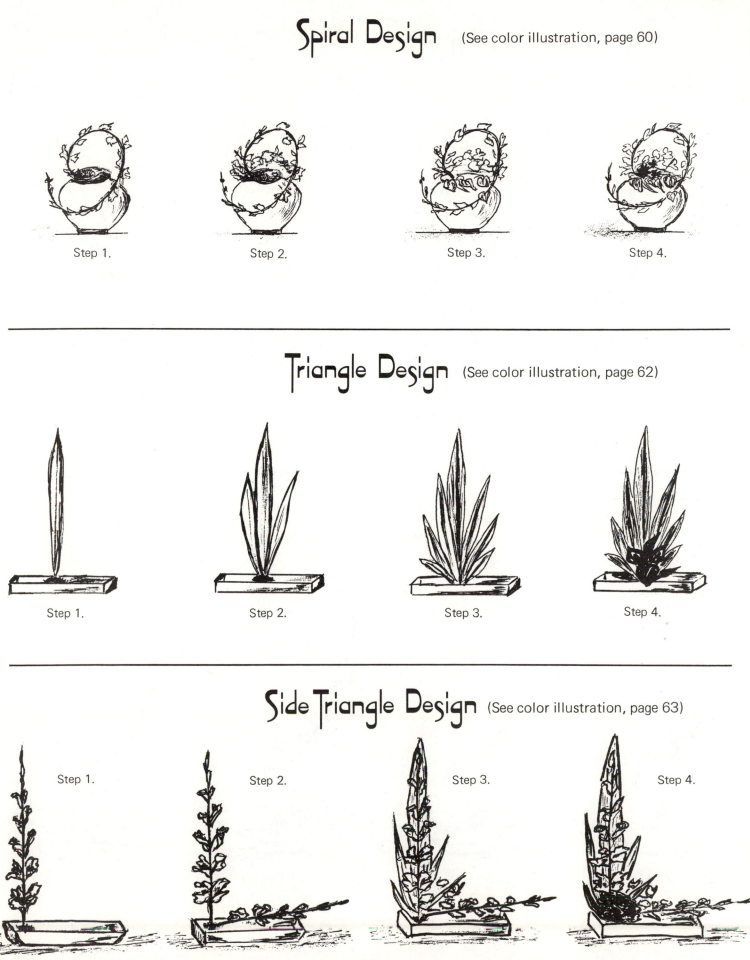

Step 1.   Step 2.   Step 3.   Step 4.

Triangle Design (See color illustration, page 62)

Step 1.   Step 2.   Step 3.   Step 4.

Side Triangle Design (See color illustration, page 63)

Step 1.   Step 2.   Step 3.   Step 4.

Hogarth Curve Design

Step 1.   Step 2.   Step 3.   Step 4.

(See color illustration, page 61)

Zig-Zag Design

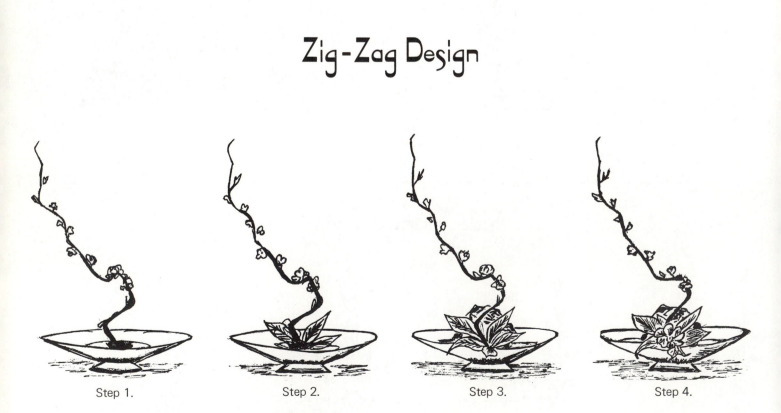

Step 1.   Step 2.   Step 3.   Step 4.

(See color illustration, page 64)

SUGGESTED SCALE OF POINTS FOR GEOMETRIC DESIGNS

Classes specifying type of Design, Color Harmony, Suitability to Placement, or Occasion.	Expressive (with title)	Decorative (without title)
Conformance	10	15
Design	35	40
Color Harmony	20	25
Distinction	15	20
Expression	20	
	100	100

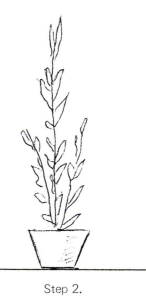

Step 1.

Step 2.

Step 3.

Step 4.

WELCOME
*A **Vertical** design suitable for an entryway or hallway, using bright orange and yellow marigolds combined with varigated New Zealand Flax.*

VERTICAL DESIGN

HORIZONTAL DESIGN

*A **Horizontal** design of dainty textures of American Linden blossoms, chrysanthemum, yellow and white daisies in an elevated container.*

Step 1.

Step 2.

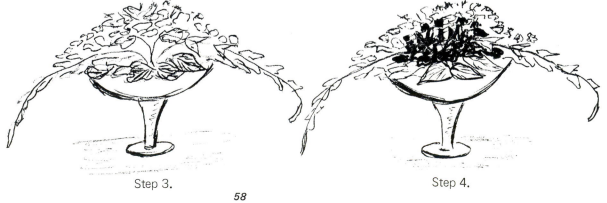

Step 3.

Step 4.

Step 1. Step 2.

CIRCLE DESIGN

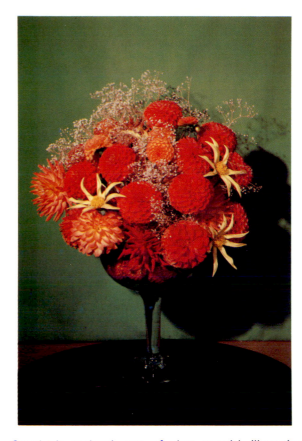

Step 3. Step 4.

Completely enclosed mass of plant material, illustrating round shape in geometric design. **Round** *form can also be achieved by a round outline such as a wire loop with design arranged within the enclosed space. Examples are shown in a later chapter on hanging designs.*

OVAL DESIGN

Step 1. Step 2.

Step 3. Step 4.

An oval *shaped design, nearly closed silhouette and most suitable as a mass design which is still popular in our homes, churches and public places today.*

CRESCENT DESIGN

Step 1.

Step 2.

Step 3.

Step 4.

The crescent *is one of the most exciting of geometric designs because the half open circle leaves room for imagination and freedom to the viewer. It is an ideal design for beginning arrangers as it is an easy lesson in gradation with inspiring results.*

The spiral *design is seldom exhibited in flower shows, yet is an interesting design and an especially good window sill companion adding fresh flowers to greenery through the winter months. A pillow vase as shown here, is a contrast to the rounded spiral form. The avocado green plate is a repetition of the rounded form.*

SPIRAL DESIGN

Step 1.

Step 2.

Step 3.

Step 4.

HOGARTH CURVE DESIGN

The Hogarth Curve, *probably the most graceful of design shapes forming a lazy "S" by reversed curved lines, was called the curve of beauty by English artist, Hogarth more than 200 years ago. It is a most inspiring design for Line or mass-line arrangements.*

Step 1.

Step 2.

Step 3.

Step 4.

TRIANGLE DESIGN

Step 1.

Step 2.

Step 3.

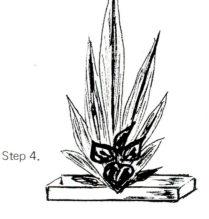

Step 4.

The triangle *is probably the easiest most basic design for beginning arrangers because it is symmetrical. Starting with the center of the design, placing the tallest spike of material in the needle holder, using gradation of spike forms down to the container on each side, sets the stage for the floral materials and the focal point. This design shape especially needs to be finished on the back side for good third dimensional quality.*

Step 1.

A side triangle *is designed from straight lines and is one step away from the symmetrical triangle. One simply shifts the center axis to the right or left of the design making it an asymmetrical triangle.*

Step 2.

Step 3.

Step 4.

DE TRIANGLE DESIGN

ZIG-ZAG DESIGN

A Zig Zag *design shape is especially nice to create in spring-time when flowering branches are available. A Zig Zag design in vivid colors in a flower show is an "eye stopper" as it is a restless, demanding design. A good lesson in direction of plant material.*

Step 1.

Step 2.

Step 3.

Step 4.

Color

D. COLOR

Color is the visual response of the eye to reflected light rays. Everything seen by the human eye is colored, including space itself. Form, shape and design are revealed by color. Design and color are ever related, as each depends on the other.

There are many different points of view in the study of Color. There are several different color theories. The important thing for flower arrangers to consider is that the art of using color in flower arrangement does not lie in the technical sense but in color as sensation as the way in which the human eye, brain, and psyche react to what is seen.

The National Council of State Garden Clubs Inc., has chosen the Pigment System of Color because of its general use, familiarity and simplicity. Also it was chosen because the color wheel of three primaries of red, yellow and blue is an equal division of warm and cool colors, whereas other circles tend to favor cool colors over warm colors. Most flowers are in the warm region of the circle and better fit the purpose of the flower arranger.

Pigment System

The pigment system is based on the fact that colors can be mixed to create new colors. All other colors can be created from the three primaries of red, yellow, and blue.

a. Equal amounts of red and yellow produce orange.
b. Equal amounts of yellow and blue produce green.
c. Equal amounts of blue and red produce violet.

Orange, green and violet are secondary colors. Between the primaries and secondaries lie many intermediates.

Neutral or Achromatic Colors: Do not have a hue.
Black
White
Gray — a combination of Black and White

In Flower Arrangement we use colors that nature provides in plant materials. We cannot mix colors to create new ones. The Pigment System shows how and why colors are related and furnished a logical system for naming colors.

Color Dimensions

Color as a design element, has three dimensions or qualities, which the designer must consider in order to use color effectively in design.

Hue — the specific name of a color.
Value — the lightness or darkness of color.
Chroma — the brightness or dullness of a color.

Hue — is a specific name of a color, such as red, orange, yellow, green, blue and violet.

Value — is the lightness or darkness of a hue.
A tint is a light value — the result of adding white.
A shade is a dark value — the result of adding black.

Chroma — is the intensity of a color. Tone is color not at full intensity. It is the result of adding gray or the complementary hue. Full chroma, bright, intense, and strong are all terms that describe pure hue.

The hue circle is composed of pure hues arranged in a circle in their natural order as in the solar spectrum (rainbow): red, orange, yellow, green, blue, violet.

The hue circle includes six intermediates:
1. red-orange (R-O)
2. yellow-orange (Y-O)
3. yellow-green (Y-G)
4. blue-green (B-G)
5. blue-violet (B-V)
6. red-violet (R-V)

The *color wheel* is composed of the hue circle expanded with gradations of light values (tints) on the outside and dark values (shades) on the inside. (See color, page 68).

The color triangle is a triangular chart of one hue with all of its modifications, showing gradations from pure hue through tints to white, tones to gray, and shades to black; also, from white through gray to black.

Color Vision

How we see color, and how color affects us, guides us in the use of color in design.

Warm — Stimulating Colors

In the hue circle, yellow through orange to red, are stimulating or strong colors. In values it is the light values, including white; in chromas, it is the intense chromas. Red and the colors which are near red, such as orange and violet-red are warm colors because we associate them with fire and heat.

Cool — Releasing Colors

The other half of the hue circle, green through blue, to violet, are releasing colors. Dark values including black, and grayed chromas including gray are also relaxing. Blue and the colors near blue are cool colors because we associate them with water, ice and sky.

Restful Colors

Colors that are between stimulating colors and releasing colors are restful. The most plentiful color in nature — leaf green — is mostly yellow-green of middle value and moderate chroma.

Additional Qualities

When several colors of the same intensity are seen from the distance, red appears nearer, blue recedes and gives a feeling of depth.

White and light colors appear larger, yet lighter in weight, while dark colors and black appear smaller yet heavier than other colors.

Light

Light is the source of all color. Without light there is no color. Both the amount and kind of light determine color. Sunlight contains visible color to the human eye. The colors we see in daylight are natural colors. Artificial light lacks various rays that produce colors; this may alter the color in an arrangement indoors with artificial light. Also darker colors inside appear to be drab compared to lighter values. This is an important consideration in exhibiting in flower shows or an arrangement for an evening function.

LIGHT HAS MANY DIMENSIONS IN FLORAL DESIGN

It is a well known fact that without light there is no color. Is it not true that light totally affects all of the other *ELEMENTS* — and all of the *PRINCIPLES* of design?

HOW LIGHT AFFECTS THE DESIGN ELEMENTS:

SPACE — Interesting solids and voids which create space within a floral design must have light to be seen. A silhouette of the design results from shadows of the light in front of the design.

LINE — Direct light on the line material in the design also creates interesting shadows resulting from light.

FORM — has more depth as the result of light.

PATTERN — must have light to show the lines, shapes, forms and spaces between as well as hues, values and chromas forming the color pattern and a more refined silhouette.

TEXTURE — is highlighted by lighting, emphasizes surface contrasts, is not visual without light.

COLOR — Light is the source of all color. There is no color without light. Both the amount and kind of light determine color. This can also include artificial light which lacks various rays that produce colors, as a result colors appear different depending on the kind of light.

HOW LIGHT AFFECTS THE DESIGN PRINCIPLES

BALANCE — The positions of lighting greatly affects the balance of a design and its silhouette and an important consideration in staging a floral design as well as the over-all lighting of a flower show.

PROPORTION — light is necessary to show the relationship of areas and amounts to each other and to the whole in a floral design.

SCALE — Light can influence the size relationship in a floral design when lighting emphasizes one special feature within the design. An example could be a small figurine appearing larger than it actually is because of direct light effects.

RHYTHM — Direct light is necessary to see the visual path through a floral design which suggests motion.

DOMINANCE — Light plays a very important role to emphasize the dominance in a design such as a spotlight on the center of interest or if a sculpture or large figurine is the dominant feature in the design.

CONTRAST — Light is essential in order to see light to dark in black and white, color values and contrasts of the other Elements of Design mentioned above.

Because floral design is basically a visual art and the Elements and Principles are totally invisable without light — it is paramount that *LIGHT* must be considered.

It is the opinion of this writer that *LIGHT* could be considered the *FIRST ELEMENT OF FLORAL DESIGN* with the six Elements of Design to follow as listed in the Handbook For Flower Shows by the National Council of State Garden Clubs, Inc.

The Color Circle

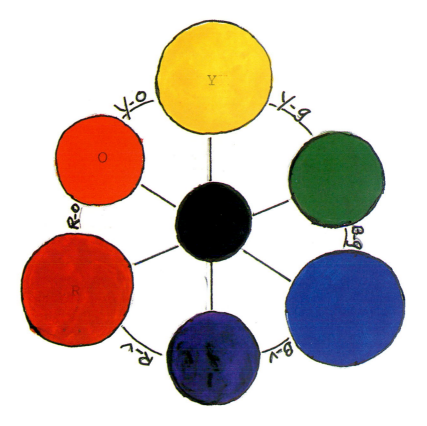

The Color Triangle

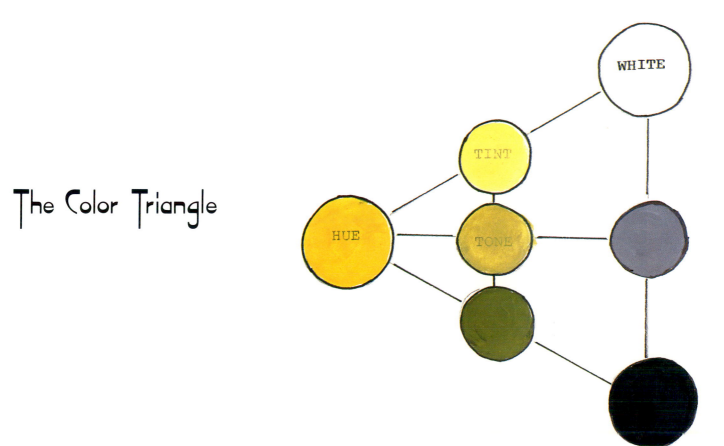

Color Dimensions

The color wheel is composed of the hue circle of pure hues arranged in a circle in their natural order as in the solar spectrum with gradations of light values (tints) and dark values (shades to the center of the wheel).

COLOR SCHEMES
Related Color Schemes

MONOCHROMATIC color scheme consists of one hue and its tints, tones and/or shades.

Each hue segment on the color wheel could result in a Monochromatic color scheme.

An ANALOGOUS color scheme consists of colors near each other on a color wheel or chart. It may include pure hues, tints, tones, and/or shades. A convenient guide is to use no less than three colors, no more than 1/3 of the color wheel and no more than one pigment primary. The illustration shows two analogous color schemes. A warm analogous color scheme using the yellow as the primary. A cool analogous color scheme using blue as the primary.

Related color schemes tend to be emotionally satisfying.

RELATED COLOR WHEEL

CONTRASTING COLOR SCHEMES

DIRECT COMPLEMENTS

A contrasting color scheme may be a contrast of hue, value, or chroma. Complementary colors are contrasting hues. These are opposites on the hue circle or color wheel. Examples:

Red and green
Orange and blue
Yellow and violet
Red-orange and blue-green
And other combinations.

SPLIT COMPLEMENT

In a Split Complement color scheme a key hue is combined with the two hues that lie next to its direct complement. Examples:

Red with yellow-green and blue-green
Green with red-orange and red violet
Blue with red-orange and yellow-orange
Violet with yellow-orange and yellow-green

DOUBLE ANALOGOUS

PAIRED COMPLEMENTS

In this color scheme, two hues are used with their direct complements. To obtain the best results, the two related hues on one side of the wheel should be of high value, or light graved chroma, while the two opposite should be of low value, or dark grayed chroma.

TRIADS

In triad color schemes three hues, equally spaced about the Color Circle are used together. Examples:
    Red — yellow — blue
        Red-orange, yellow-green and blue-violet
        Yellow-orange, blue-green and red-violet

OTHER CONTRASTING COLOR SCHEMES

ADJACENT COMPLEMENTARY: Three hues: the basic hue, its direct complement, and either of the splits.

ANALOGOUS COMPLEMENTARY: Four hues: three hues adjacent on the wheel, with the direct complement of any one of them.

NEAR COMPLEMENTARY: Two hues: the basic hue, with either of the splits.

In a class calling for a specific color scheme, every hue falling within the designated formula *must be represented in the plant material.* The container *alone* cannot constitute one of the needed hues.

Selecting colors that are related or contrasting is a first step in achieving a color harmony. The selected colors are then organized according to the principles of design.

EXAMPLES OF CONTRASTING COLOR SCHEMES:

DIRECT COMPLEMENTS

SPLIT COMPLEMENT

PAIRED COMPLEMENT

TRIAD

Wild grasses gathered from the roadside are combined with orange chrysanthemums in an analogous color scheme.

Tints, tones and shades or redviolet of lilac, rhododendrons and allium are combined in this Hogarth massed line design. The container is a Grecian urn in neutral black to conform with the monochromatic color study and dark violet tulips.

A tall **massed-line** *design in an analogous color study of red-orange to yellow-orange. The pottery container is a subdued value of orange with white overglaze that spills into free form patterns into deeper tones of brown. Pampas grass, smoke tree and manzanita branch form the outline and silhouette of the design. The design is framed by a 2½ x 6 foot natural wood panel. The flowers are chrysanthemums and dahlias.*

This interesting fasciated mullen found near Bend, Oregon forms pleasing space relations to the monochromatic color study. Dried stalks of Darlingtonia support the heavy rough texture of the mullen. Orange dahlias, astilbe and a fungus, complete the design in a free form brown rough textured container. The bamboo raft carries out a lighter value of orange to complete the color study.

A **vertical** *design in an analogous color scheme of orange, yellow-orange, yellow and yellow-green. Plant materials are varigated flax, scotchbroom, magnolia leaves, yellow and orange dahlias in a bullet-shaped container to give a smooth transition to the slender vertical design.*

A direct complement color study of yellow and purple. The heavy massed line is a Hogarth Curve of yellow daisies, Dutch iris, lilac, alium, tulips, and spirea.

The massed design to the left is a triadic color scheme using the three primaries of yellow, red and blue in various degrees of intensity. The blue delphinium is the fullest chroma combined with pink chiffon poppies, yellow daisies, yellow dahlias and pale blue to white hydrangea. The background color is one of the colors used in the color scheme.

An analogous color harmony in red, red-violet and violet using rhododendrons, lilacs and spirea.

Luster is achieved when small touches of exceedingly pure color are introduced to shade to black using a black or dark rich background. The two hanging designs of dark red dahlias are given a luster effect by adding glistening babybreath. Seaweed painted black brings the two designs together with interesting enclosed space.

(See other examples of Luster & Irridescence in Aerial Design)

New Visual Experiences

COLOR AND LIGHT

The Effect of Luster

Where there are color sequences from pure color, to shade, to black, highly lustrous effects become possible. It is necessary for the background to be black or a deep, rich shade. Such colors may also be in the flower arrangement itself.

Luster is achieved when small touches of exceedingly pure color are then introduced. All white, neutral gray, and all pastel colors must be eliminated.

The Effect of Iridescence

The effect of Iridescence can best be explained as a play of colors producing rainbow effects such as in soap bubbles or the inside of an abalone shell, the rainbow colors with a silvery background. The sequence is toward gray or toward neutral tones. The background for the arrangement should be limited to soft colors such as rose, beige, sage green, tan, grayish blue, orchid or lavender. These may also be a part of the flower arrangement.

Iridescence is achieved when small touches of very pure color are added to pastels which are natural to many flowers. The pastels must be fairly vivid, and they must be somewhat lighter in value or brightness than the other colors in the composition and the background.

The Effect of Chromatic Light

To achieve chromatic light effects, a color harmony is studied as it appears under colored light (or through a sheet of cellophane). This appearance is then duplicated or approximated with real flowers, vases, background or other props.

COLOR AVANT GARDE

In recent years, great advances have been made in creativity in floral design. I have often wondered why we have not made the same move forward in more advanced color studies. Too often our flower show schedules state ''an arrangement featuring one color.'' The comment is often heard ''color classes are too difficult for new arrangers or for the public to understand.'' If we would make an effort to schedule more color studies in our shows our future arrangers and public would begin to recognize them. When flowers are in abundance in spring and summer, it is exciting to try new color schemes.

It is time advanced arrangers moved forward into avant garde color studies in the effects of luster, iridescence, etc. It is an exciting challenge and refreshing to create a color scheme you have never made before. As long as the design is good and has good color harmony, who is to say you cannot create a double analogous, a triple direct complement and many other exciting color schemes. Think how beautiful a flower show scheduling only color studies would be. It is a new idea in the right direction and I hope more garden clubs will take up this challenge to greater color dimensions.

An unusual color study — a double direct complement in hues of nearly equal value of — red orange / blue green — red violet / yellow green.
Yellow green is anise, evergreen and salal. Blue green — juniper, red orange — dahlias, red violet — smoke tree foliage.

Exciting color contrasts are illustrated in this massed-line design. Colors range from deep true violet of the delphinium, red violet in the maple leaves and the container, variations of yellows in the dahlias and wheat, combined with red-orange dahlias. This design is not intended to conform to any of the contrasting color studies. It was designed to show how exciting color combinations can be achieved. There is no rule that you cannot combine any colors you choose, as long as they are harmonious and you are not conforming to a flower show schedule.

The effect of iridescence is achieved in this design by using small amounts of pure bright pastels with a larger amount of soft greyed plant materials producing a silvery effect as that in the accompanying abalone shell. The crystal container is compatible with the dainty textures and adds sparkle to the design. The background fabric is heavy silvery grey satin which also adds to the iridescency.

SUGGESTED SCALE OF POINTS FOR DESIGN CLASSES

Classes specifying type of Design, Color Harmony, Suitability to Placement, or Occasion.

Monochromatic
Analogous
Direct Complement
Split Complement
Paired Complement
Triad

	Expressive (with title)	Decorative (without title)
Conformance	10	15
Design	35	40
Color Harmony	20	25
Distinction	15	20
Expression	20	
	100	100

Summary

Think in Units of Three's

1. Three Main Divisions of Design
    1. Elements
    2. Principles
    3. Attributes

2. Three Basic Geometric Shapes of Design
    1. Cube
    2. Sphere
    3. Triangle

3. Three main Types of Conventional Design Today
    1. Line — Oriental Influence
    2. Mass — Occidental Influence
    3. Mass-Line — American Origin

4. Types of Plant Materials Used in Flower Arrangement
    1. Line Materials — for skeleton of design
    2. Round forms — for focal point
    3. Fillers — for gradation, depth etc.

5. The Color Triangle

1. Hue	1. Tint	1. White
2. Value	2. Tone	2. Gray
3. Chroma	3. Shade	3. Black

1. Primary Colors — Red, Yellow, Blue
2. Secondary Colors — Green, Orange, Violet
3. Intermediate Colors — Combinations of primary and secondary colors.

Part 3

Miniature Designs

Miniature designs are a reproduction of an average size arrangement. It conforms to all principles of design, except that it is greatly reduced in scale. A miniature must not exceed 5 inches in any dimension.

Plant materials must be naturally small and dainty in size. There is a surprisingly good selection of small flowers or florets that work very effectively for miniatures. One must avoid using one bright large flower as a center of interest which gives a "bulls eye" effect.

One of the most common faults of miniatures in flower shows is that the container is too large for the amount of plant material, either affecting the proportion or the overall size of the design which must be five inches or less in all dimensions in a standard flower show. Small bases also enhance the design.

Miniatures are best staged at eye level in individual squares or miniature niches with consideration given to background colors the same as a design in a large niche. The niches should be well lighted for judging and display.

Another attractive way to stage miniatures is on small graduated free form tables at table level or slightly higher with the same considerations for color and light.

Suggestions for miniature containers are:

a. thimble
b. small sea shells
c. nut shells
d. small bottle caps
e. plastic grape molds
f. miniature vases
g. bird egg
h. seed pods
i. miniature tea sets
j. driftwood
k. stones
l. buttons

SUGGESTED SCALE OF POINTS FOR MINIATURES

	Expressive (with title)	Decorative (without title)
Scale	35	35
Design (All other principles)	25	35
Color Harmony	10	15
Distinction	15	15
Expression	15	
	100	100

Small Arrangements

Small arrangements are very versatile today in flower shows and in our homes. With living space becoming more limited in our homes, apartments and mobile homes, the small arrangement is very satisfactory for floral decoration. Another good requirement of small arrangements is that they do not require as many flowers to make. This is an advantage to arrangers who may not have a large selection of plant materials or new arrangers just learning artistic design. They are also a good arrangement class for beginning arrangers to try as they have few restrictions and are fairly easy to make.

The main considerations you will want to know about small designs for exhibiting in a standard flower show are:
1. The arrangement must not exceed eight inches in any dimension.
2. Average plant materials may be used with consideration given to space alloted.
3. Plant material must be in proportion to the size of the container. Example: Carnations would be more in proportion to the container more than if a large dahlia bloom was used.

Following are some interesting ways to use small arrangements:
1. Exhibited in a standard flower show.
2. Small coffee table.
3. Windowsill.
4. Bookcase shelf.
5. Take to a friend in the hospital, convalescent home, retirement home.

Another interesting approach to small design is to use them in several units as a dining table center piece. If the table is small and set for two people, two paired arrangements of unequal size can be very effective. For a larger table, perhaps three to five units of small designs used together would be exciting. Thought should be given to space allowed on the table, design in each of the arrangements, compatible containers, either using materials very nearly alike or contrasts for interest. Color harmony and textures relating to other table appointments should be considered.

Corsages

Corsages are plant material arranged according to the principles of design for personal adornment. Considerations should be give to:
1. Occasion — Daytime or Evening.
2. Background — Color, texture.
3. Size — according to person wearing it.

Corsages may be made of fresh plant material, dried plant material or a combination of both.

In a Flower Show, corsages should be staged at eye level.

Corsages are a carry-over of personal adornment worn in the Grecian Period when people wore an olive branch on their lapel.

(See color illustrations, page 82)

SUGGESTED SCALE OF POINTS FOR SMALL ARRANGEMENTS

Classes specifying type of Design, Color Harmony, Suitability to Placement, or Occasion.	Expressive (with title)	Decorative (without title)
Conformance	10	15
Design	35	40
Color Harmony	20	25
Distinction	15	20
Expression	20	
	100	100

Flower Show Table Settings

Definition of Terminology for Flower Show Tables

Decorative Unit

The decorative unit can be either the flower arrangement or the arrangement plus accessories. The container, flowers, fruits or other plant material must be related in texture, color and quality. Coordination of the overall effect of the table setting can be achieved if the decorative unit emphasizes a hue which is subordinate in the china. The decorative unit generally occupies not over one-third of the table's length. It should be placed where it will be most effective in the general seating plan either at the end of a table if the table is placed against a wall or low enough so guests can see over it. The decorative unit must be finished all around when placed in the middle of a dining table. If against a wall it should be finished enough to give good depth.

Accessories

Can be anything in an arrangement in addition to plant material, container, base, background or mechanics which are subordiante in the design. The flower show schedule should determine what accessory(s) would be appropriate for a specific class. Accessories may be used singly or in pairs. They are most often used on a buffet table, luncheon table or a large refreshment table where candles are not used. Accessories may be used on a dinner table but are less frequently used. They should be related to the decorative unit in such a way that they do not crowd the setting nor detract from the decorative unit or the overall design of the table setting.

Dishes

When individual place settings are required, the place plate becomes the **keynote** because its repetitive use makes it dominant. It governs the color, pattern and quality of all other appointments. Dishes include plates, cups, saucers and serving pieces. Depending on the flower show schedule as to theme or occasion, they may be fine china, pottery, enamel, plastic, paper or dishes from other countries.

Table Covering

The background for a table setting consists of a cloth, place mats or the bare table surface. Tablecloths or mats can be used for formal or informal occasions, depending upon their quality and texture. Contrast is an important consideration in combining china with the tablecloth. if the china has a prominant or multi-colored pattern, it is best to use a table cloth of one of the colors in the place plate. If the china is on one color, the opposite approach of a printed cloth gives interesting contrast.

Place Mats

Place mats should not overlap. Adequate spacing allows 24 inches from the center of one place setting to the center of the one beside it. Place mats may be used on a bare table or placed on an overall table covering for color emphasis and unity to the overall table setting. Consideration must be given to the texture, color and quality of the place mats according to the table covering.

Appointments

Appointments include necessary items for dining such as table coverings, napkins, dishes, glassware, serving pieces and candles.

Candles

Candles are not used on luncheon tables except where there is inadequate light. They may be used on all dinner tables, patio and tea tables when needed. At a seated meal the flame should not be at eye level.

Flat Silver or **food stuffs** such as mints and nuts are not recommended for flower show tables.

(See color illustrations, pages 83 — 85)

Table Classes

Table Exhibits in a Standard Flower Show may be exhibited as an entire section or one or two classes may be included in the design sections.

If a Top Award is to be given in a table section, there must be at least three classes with four entries in each class. The required number of entries may include classes for:
1. Dining tables.
2. Refreshment tables.
3. Coffee tables.

An important factor in all types of table exhibits is the coordination of the decorative unit and table appointments within the space allowed.

The Flower Show schedule must specify:
1. Type and purpose of table.
2. Number of place settings required.
3. Size of space allowed in all table classes.

A Standard Flower Show may have two types of table exhibits:
1. Functional
2. Exhibition

A Functional Table is a table exhibit arranged for the **the service of food.** It will include:
1. Dishes
2. Linens — cloth, and/or placemats and napkins.
3. Decorative unit — with or without accessories.

An Exhibition Table is for exhibition purposes only and is not related to the actual service of food. The elements and principles of design govern the selection and placement of appointments and decorative unit within the space allowed.

Exhibition tables may be staged in niches, on individual tables or several on a display table with or without background.

The Following Table Classes can be *Functional* or *Exhibitional.*

Semi-Formal Table:

Patterned closely after the formal dinner table.

If functional: an even number of place settings are symmetrically placed with the decorative unit designed to permit conversation across the functional table. Accessory(s) may be used.

Informal Table:

This style includes breakfast, brunch, lunch, supper, family dinner, outdoor and patio tables. The Functional informal table may consist of even or uneven number of place settings. The decorative unit is placed in any area where it will not hinder conversation.

Buffet Table:

The buffet table is informal in character, regardless of the occasion, the quality or placement of appointments. If functional, ease of service is an important consideration. Serving dishes should be shown with individual plates or bowls, conveniently placed for the course indicated. Table appointments should not be crowded, but arranged for ease of service. For exhibition purposes, a service for at least five is necessary for a Functional Buffet table.

Reception Tables:

Reception tables may be formal or informal, depending on the occasion. These are similar to a buffet table in consideration to ease of service and placement of table appointments.

TV and Breakfast Trays:

Trays, especially breakfast or convalescent trays call for fresh plant material of cheerful colors. The decorative unit should be stable for carrying purposes. The tray should be arranged for ease of self service and never crowded. Since the tray will be viewed up close and in a small space, color harmony, texture and design is of utmost importance.

SUGGESTED SCALE OF POINTS

Functional Tables		
Functionalism	15	15
Decorative unit	20	25
Design	15	15
Color and Textural Harmony . . .	20	25
Distinction	15	20
Expression	15	
	100	100

Exhibition Tables	Expressive (with title)	Decorative (without title)
Conformance	10	15
Design	30	35
Color and Textural Harmony . .	25	30
Distinction	15	20
Expression	20	
	100	100

OTHER SUGGESTED DESIGN CATEGORIES SUITABLE
FOR FLOWER SHOWS AND SYMPOSIUMS.

PLAQUES — are usually designs in low relief with dried plant material and differ from collage in that material is usually arranged conventionally or in a natural growth pattern attached to a panel and are wall hung. Plaques may include other low relief natural materials such as sea shells, or stones. Plaques are suitable in the home as well as in flower shows and symposiums.

STILL LIFE EXHIBIT — in contrast to an assemblage, is usually realistic in feeling while an assemblage may be abstract. A Still Life tells a story or a theme and is interpreted through the use of objects in their true size rather than by the choice and dominance of plant materials used. Still life paintings are good examples for the arranger to follow.

A SHADOW BOX DESIGN — is an arrangement of plant material shown outlined against a foreground of translucent material by use of lighting behind it. Special lighting effects with color can be an exciting challenge to the arranger. Condition of the plant material, texture and color are irrelevant because the material is viewed as a silhouette rather than the actual plant material. The elements of space, line, form, size and pattern are essential to a true Shadow Box design.

CHRISTMAS SHOWS — mainly feature such decorations as wreathes, swags, garlands, kissing balls, door decorations, Christmas trees and decorated packages but may also have holiday table classes, mantel arrangements, and other Christmas designs suitable throughout the home.

OP — ART — can be best expressed by the term bizaare, that which is strikingly out of the ordinary. A design which demands visual perception through the use of aggressive forms of equal strength, equal hue, and equal luminosity. The design may include soft sculpture, bold colors and eclectic unrelated objects. It must contain some fresh or dry plant material and have a quality of beauty as all other floral design categories.

CHURCH ARRANGEMENTS — are governed by the symbolism and restrictions of the individual religions. The architecture of the sanctuary, color, placement and symbolism which would include seasons must be considered in making church floral designs. Mass or mass-line designs reflecting a rich formal dignity from the past are usually used in most churches today.

Miniatures

Small Design Arrangements

Table Settings

"Hospitality Today" — *An Exhibition Segment table illustrates a setting suited to todays living. The poppies on the Desert Flower china are compatible with the rough textured informal grass fans and are repeated in bright orange oriental poppies as fresh plant material. The bright orange runner ties the table setting together.*

"A BRIGHT NEW DAY" *Informal breakfast table setting for two. Color contrasts are as vibrant as the morning with white china on a bright green cloth with green and white table accessories. The bright orange Oriental poppies and grasses in a low black dish are enriched by two orange placemats.*

SPRING NOSTALGIA — *an informal luncheon table for two with spring garden flowers repeating colors in the print cloth over lace. Light green placemats with bright green napkins accent the heavy crystal salad bowls. Matching salad bowl and tulip shaped goblets complete the table setting.*

SUMMER EVENING — *a semi-formal table setting for service of six. The white china with rose pattern is enriched by the pale pink lace tablecloth and a centerpiece of pink and red roses. Crystal goblets and pink candles in crystal candleabra complete the table appointments.*

COFFEE HOUR. *An informal table setting for a small reception. Bavarian china in the moss rose pattern is appropriate with the German lace linen table cloth. The floral centerpiece is a mixed garden bouquet of flowers as dainty as the pattern in the coffee-tea set. Pink napkins are highlighted with individual rose buds.*

Free Form Designs

A five foot tall design created from the roots of a tree which was cut horizontally to make a six inch thick naturalistic wood screen with solid and negative spaces. Large red and orange dahlias and scotchbroom add color and height to the design.

Free-Form branches and tree root with enclosed space is the structural form of this free-form design. The design unit is supported by a heavy metal rod raised from a metal base to add height and give the design more interest.

One large limb enclosing negative space is visually softened with bamboo and scotchbroom with a large white cactus dahlia, smaller red and yellow dahlias for color. The wood is raised from the base by a heavy metal rod drilled into the wood.

"By The Sea" — *This beautiful piece of driftwood is used in its naturalistic state, with sea grass, wild beach flowers, floats and fish net on a free form base.*

The same piece of driftwood left to the elements was turned upside down and mounted on a metal rod and base and exhibited at the Coos County Fair under the scheduled title "Ocean Frontiers".

"Earth's Own Sculptor" — *Sculptured by earth's elements, this spectacular weathered wood is most effective raised from a base. A metal rod is welded to this heavy angle iron base to support the heavy wood. Plant materials are dahlias and smoke tree foliage.*

"Trout Season" — *A huge knot of weathered wood found in the sand dunes at Coos Bay, Oregon makes an excellent container resembling a trout creel for this vertical mass-line design using spring flowers. The slender bamboo poles suggest fish poles. The bamboo raft suggests water.*

Part 4

Creativity

We should be as creative as we can with the wise choice of plant materials as our elements according to the Principles of design with the thought that we are horticulturists and our art form should always give emphasis to the use of fresh plant materials to achieve the attributes of design.

"Man's mind, stretched to a new idea, never goes back to its original dimension."

Creativity

I. What is Creativity?

Creativity is organized knowledge gathered from the past, used according to the principles of design with the ingenuity to see and to implement ordinary objects into something new and beautiful. Creativity in floral design can be objective or non-objective which means it can tell a story or it may be viewed for pure lines, colors, textures, space relations and forms.

a. Types of Creativity
1. Functional creativity for progress in the commercial world through inventing new products with the purpose based on profit.
2. Creativity in the fine arts for aesthetic pleasure. This kind of creativity is less realistic, it is built on the imaginary with emphasis on beauty.

II. Let Us Analyze the Creative Person

The creative person is more sensitive, more cultivated, yet more primitive, more destructive, somewhat madder but a lot saner than the average person!

The more creative you are, the less likely you are to be concerned with impressing others or keeping up with the Joneses. As revealed by creativity research at the National Institute of Mental Health, it was found that people who made high scores on creativity tests tended to be the least concerned with making a favorable impression on others. They also differed from less creative people in that they were more poised, spontaneous, more adventurous, humorous, rebellious and assertive. Creative people have less patience for detail and following directions, they like to think imaginatively rather than logically. They do not make good accountants or bookkeepers.

Creativity is like being on the brink of a waterfall. It is something totally yours — right now! It is your interpretation, the final statement must be yours. It is your challenge and decision if it is a good design. Creativity is adventure, it is daring and the unknown.

"Courage is that inherent human quality which counts most. Courage to act on your own knowledge of the past to strive for the future. That is the only creative reserve any of us have."

Certainly it is difficult! Anything new is not going to be easy and guaranteed to be perfect the first time. Challenge is a healthy attitude. You would feel no sense of satisfaction to do the same thing you have done over and over again or something you have seen before or copied. That is not creativity!

"To be no one — but yourself, alone in a world rotating by the force of conformity is the hardest creative battle which anyone can fight; and never stop fighting for self identity."

III. Ways to Approach Creativity

1. **Positive Thinking** — Whatever your goal may be, keep in mind that nothing is impossible for you. Do not worry about how your goal will be achieved. Simply keep in mind the end result. "What man can conceive, he can achieve". The most imaginative people are the most credulous, for to them, everything is possible.
2. **Mind Control**
Our mind has four depths:
Delta — unconscious
Theta — inner consciousness with dreaming or deepest meditation.
Alpha — inner consciousness associated with deep concentration, day dreaming — creativity.
Beta — everyday life, waking activities, reality.

Put your Alpha to work for you, look into your crystal ball of creative thoughts. What forms, lines, colors, spaces do you see? What mood are you in? What kind of a day is it, what kind of clouds in the sky? Some people so repress their creative ability that it only manifests itself when they are asleep. Look around your surroundings for objects that could be incorporated into a creative design.

As human beings, we have three ego states: child, adult and parent.

Child Ego State — A child sees the world as it is. The mind has not yet been cluttered with the cares, worries and restrictions of the world. We are taught to conform very early in life, to color within the lines. That is why it is so hard to break out of our shells and be individuals again. Look at the world as a child, from all angles, upside down, forward, backwards. Look at textures up close.

Study silhouettes of positive and negative spaces in plant materials, trees, mountains, forests, river beds, rocks, clouds, etc. Erase your mind of the ordinary. Learn to see objects removed from their natural frame of reference; see it for what it *is not.* So what? It is a wet burlap sack on the beach in the bright morning sun all aglitter with silvery lines and interesting black negative spaces. It is beautiful! As one of my art teachers kept repeating, "see what is really going on".

3. *Generalization, Variety* and *Flexibility* — are essential tools for creativity. We invent from memory. It has been said that what we do artistically, is a reflection of many images we have subconsciously seen in the past. Now as arrangers we select and choose from our past visual experiences to create new images. The statement was made in 1825 that generalization is necessary to the advancement of knowledge, but particularly it is indispensable to the creations of the imagination. One must reach out in many directions and often change ones mind before achieving the final result. If your design turns out to be different from your original plan, it may be better and more exciting. As long as it is good according to the principles of design. These are the thrills of creativity.

4. *Knowledge* — we must have a thorough understanding of the Principles of design and how to effectively apply them to the Elements of design to achieve the attributes of design.

5. *Experience* — Knowledge and experience work hand in hand in the physical application of plant materials, using the basic geometric design shapes as beginning arrangers to be practiced many times to achieve perfection according to the specific guidelines of geometric designs. The eye is trained by actual experience of arranging plant materials according to the elements and the principles of design. In all creative arranging, the arranger sets their own guidelines from past experiences to create non geometric designs. Good design is the responsibility of the arranger.

6. *Courage* — Through knowledge and experience one learns to have courage in ones self. It takes courage to be a real winner, as new ways are often uncertain ways. Have courage to "do your own thing".

Don't be afraid to be different and present your creativity in the manner and style that best fits you. Creativity is not a mysterious process. It is rooted in the very nature of all of us. It is the wonderful combination of environment and intelligence of action and reaction, which sets each one of us apart as someone special. The creative spirit is a fearless ability to attempt new things, tapping our past for resources to bring forth that which is new and different.

Thoughts from the past teach us a lesson on courage and creativity. It was said in 1302, "All has been discovered that can be discovered." In 1880 it was suggested that the patent office be closed because man had gone to the limit of his creativity and the things he could use. Some people still do not believe we have landed on the moon. In 1978 people were ridiculing the thought that other forms of life can be circling our earth. It is human nature to want to "put down" that which is unfamiliar or unknown.

I remember the embarassing ridicule I received at my first attempt at an abstract design a number of years ago. When I had finished my design at a Garden Club District Conference, a young viewer stepped up to me and said, "And you are a judge?" "I wouldn't be proud of that if I were you". The design was arranged on three graduated free form glass palettes with spring branches, camellias and a large round thick tuft of spring green moss. She was really convinced when the floral clay came unglued and the whole design toppled off of the glass palettes during the morning session. I quietly said to myself, "no one else in this room of some 200 gardeners had courage to try such a design," so I carefully put it back together, praying it would stay put the rest of the day. It did, and I felt I had crossed a new threshold of courage and creativity.

Creativity has been around since the beginning of time. But it is surprising the number of people today who do not understand or appreciate it.

I have found in the business world where money is the "action word", and thinking is logic rather than imaginary, creativity is not welcome or recognized. That is because "the eyes can see only what the mind can understand and finds of interest."

The Five Senses
  And How They are Related to
  Flower Arrangement

1. *Sight* —
   Our eyes are the direct pathway to expression. Through sight we are able to enjoy beauty of space, lines, forms, textures, patterns, and most exciting of all is color.

2. *Touch* —
   We first think of the physical contact of different textures when we think of touch. We compare the smooth satin surface of a rose petal to very contrasting rough granite boulders. Touch can also be the satisfaction of the actual physical work of putting an arrangement together.

3. *Smell* —
   Is there any more heavenly scent than the many mingled scents of a flower show. The scent of a lovely flower is God's gift to everyone, young or old, blind or deaf, and yet it costs so little. More people should stop to smell the flowers in this busy commercialized world.

4. *Taste* —
   No, we don't eat the daisies, but many interesting recipes do include violets, mint leaves, rose petal jelly, but taste can be thought of in another way in flower arranging — good, bad or indifferent. Good taste is appropriateness, color harmony, pleasing texture contrasts just to mention a few of many examples. Color has a great influence associated with taste, such as orange, lemon, lime, chocolate, etc., which subconsciously makes us like or dislike certain colors.
   Closely related to good taste is style:
   Style is taste and logic.
   Style is the right ground cover in the right garden.
   Style is the right arrangement in the right room with appropriate colors, textures and room appointments.
   A Cole Porter tune, the Golden Gate Bridge have style.
   Style is also closely related to creativity as style is self identification. Originality and self identification are closely related. To acquire taste is not to possess style, yet style is ever tasteful. The quality of style as in design may be unexplainable, but it

is readily identifiable. We sense it when we see it. Style as related to abstract design is the omission of the obvious. Style is the unique personal statement — the individual sparkle in a routine world. Style is courage, style is the free spirit.

   "She couldn't sketch or even draw, but designed a dress by draping the fabric on a model — and then attacking it with a large pair of scissors and a mouthful of pins. The waste was considerable but the results were fabulous — that is style."

5. *Sound* —
   Not only the fifth sense, I consider it also the sixth dimension. 1. Height, 2. Width, 3. Depth, 4. Color, 5. Light, 6. Sound. Music can influence a design through exciting dimensions of sound intensity from loud to soft, color association through music and sound, sound in relation to many different things, such as the dissident sounds of malfunctions in a rocket-ship brings the design to life as if you are in that spaceship heading for the moon into unknown space.
   Visual patterns of repetition in sound can carry out the repetition of plant materials, lines, spaces and color in a design. Sound adds depth, action, happiness, anxiety, sadness, inspiration and many other moods with more emphatic emphases than any of the other human senses.

Examples of music added to floral design is shown in the Assemblage "April in Portugal". The song "April in Portugal" accompanying the assemblage, makes one feel as if they are on the veranda overlooking the village and the smell of spring blooms on a lovely April day. Other examples of music accompanying design are illustrated in later chapters.

Thoughts on Creativity

Speak with your heart and soul — not with your lips — that is creativity.

The artist finds the greatest pleasure in painting the picture rather than viewing the work when it is finished.

The creative artist is already thinking about his next composition because he was not satisfied with his previous one.

There should be a dash of the amateur in criticism, for the amateur has the enthusiasm for adventure and is not settled down into narrow habits.

Only paper roses are afraid of the rain. We are not afraid of the enriching rain of criticism because with it will flourish our magnificent garden.

Only those who cannot create, tear to pieces the work of others.

"Constructive criticism is the salt of the earth. Destructive criticism is the deterioration of the soul."

Marie Miller

The artist is a cut above the critic, for the artist is writing something which will move the critic. The critic is writing something which will move everyone but the artist.

— Author unknown

A critic is one who knows the way but can't drive the car.

"He can see a louse as far away as China but is unconscious of an elephant on his nose."

Malay Proverb

Take Time to Think Creativity

You may say that is easier said than done. Time is like money. Ten minutes here, a dime there — it all adds up. You can spend it foolishly worrying about something you cannot control or change or you can allot yourself a certain time each day — even if it is but for a few minutes to unclutter your mind of the workaday world to give yourself a special mental treat. If you do not do this, no one else is going to give it to you. Happy thoughts are little gifts you give to yourself.

Inspiration generated from creative thoughts can be a powerful, beautiful inner peace and satisfaction to the creative person.

Free Form Design

Free form follows natures rules with irregular fluid contours which do not conform to any specifically defined geometric patterns. Free form is made up of ever changing curved lines, informal in shape and suggests organic life patterns in plant and animal life such as the human heart, the one celled amoeba, rounded fungus growths found on wood, the natural growth of plant materials and free flowing lines found in drift or weathered woods and many dainty branch patterns. Other examples of free form may be found in other concepts such as tide pools, windswept sand dunes with soft rounded forms like melting ice cream, free form pools found in the sand dunes created by wind, water and sand, high elevation lakes surrounded by free form areas of snow melting to the water's edge. Examples are endless in nature, giving great opportunities for ideas to the creative arranger.

Free form tends to have natural balance developed from natural upright growth pattern unless influenced by natures elements such as windswept pine trees on a rocky cliff.

Balance within the free form design is asymmetrical, irregular, with curved lines which are free flowing, easy, not bound and no indication of discipline as found in geometric design. There should be a continuous flow from one part of the design to another without interruptions. If lines are intercepted by too many straight lines, the design is no longer free form. As in line design, restraint must be exercised, otherwise plant materials will confuse the free flowing movement of the free form structure. Line may be intertwined to strengthen the design but must be restful and should have one direction.

Free form is considered to be a line of simplicity, of beauty and nature. It has unity from within, projecting an inner force which radiates out into freedom of undetermined boundaries. Interesting space variations can be achieved without the design losing its unified self identity.

Free form design can be objective or non-objective. One can enjoy the design for pure line, space, form, pattern, color, texture and its vivaciousness, or it can communicate a message to the viewer as an objective and interpretive design.

Movement within the design is as important as its visual attributes. Movement is created by the tension points of expanding, contracting with push and pull effects with evident circulation of movement ever present. The design seems to radiate out from its nucleus in unexpected exciting space areas similar to the ever changing action of a mobile. Depth in the design is very important.

Although informal in appearance, with no definite front, back or sides to the design, the principles of design are ever present and must be skillfully handled in this 20th Century design.

Free form design should rate high in creativity and distinction, project boldness and vitality of the 20th Century.

Free form design is highly creative, it is synonymous with Creative design except that it does not include abstract design. It is exciting and as restful as nature itself, because it is ever changing as with the shadows of the sun. Nothing is ever exactly alike because it is not man made. Free form in all aspects is natures true gift to the arranger who has the imagination and ability to create the most inspiring designs for today and tomorrow.

According to the 1977 edition of the Handbook for Flower Shows by the National Council of State Garden Clubs, Inc., the classification, Free-Form, has a broader meaning than was designated by that term before. Free-Form now encompasses those designs that developed in the transition from the Conventional to the Abstract. These were called: Modern, Contemporary, Free-Style and Free-Form. Now, Free-Form refers not only to free-flowing designs but all designs developed since Conventional *except* Abstract. "Any design that is not Traditional, Conventional or Abstract is now classified as Free-Form."

SUGGESTED SCALE OF POINTS FOR FREE-FORM DESIGN

Classes eligible for Creativity Award	Expressive (with title)	Decorative (without title)
Conformance	10	10
Design	25	35
Color	15	15
Distinction	15	20
Creativity — Originality	20	20
Expression	15	
	100	100

Driftwood & Weathered Wood

INTRODUCTION

Driftwood or weathered wood, determined by whether it is water washed by ocean, river or lakes or if it is weathered by earths elements of wind, sun, rain, sand and rocks, is one of the most exciting and challenging materials for flower arrangers, as each piece of wood is original, never any two alike.

One learns to let the wood suggest the line, rhythm, textures and interesting spaces within the wood. Being free form of a naturalistic nature, drift or weathered wood gives endless variety and opportunities for exciting creative designs.

CREATIVE WAYS WITH
DRIFTWOOD OR WEATHERED WOOD

Creativity has brought a new look and exciting approaches to arranging with weathered woods. As arrangements have become larger and taller to fit our homes today, the use of weathered wood has also taken on new dimensions. It is not uncommon to use wood as tall as a person. Lovely sculptural free standing specimens such as the one shown on page 85 are for the driftwood hunters search along the Pacific Coast. The skeletal remains of a tree are carefully groomed by nature to bring out its strongest character, leaving interesting spaces to enhance the wood.

Simplicity is achieved in the choice of plant materials used and the restraint in the placement so as not to take away from the interesting solids and spaces.

Bold flower forms are natural with driftwood in creative design. Such flowers as dahlias, lilies, hibiscus, orchids, torch ginger, water lilies and dozens of others give the dynamic striking effect needed in creative design. Many dry materials in bold form such as sun flowers, artichoke, and hydrangeas, are also suitable to incorporate in driftwood designs.

Whether it is driftwood, which is water washed by ocean, lakes, rivers, etc., or weathered wood which has been exposed to earths elements of sun, wind, rain, sand, etc., all wood is very versatile. It can be used in a miniature design of five to eight inches or in a much larger scale of an assemblage as much as five to eight feet tall. All elements of design can be present in driftwood; space, line, form, pattern, texture and color which enhance plant materials combined with the wood.

Each piece of drift or weathered wood possesses its own character and originality which lends great opportunity to the arranger to create a fresh new image never seen before. There is great variety to be discovered under the terms of drift or weathered wood. Many of my choice wood specimens have been found in the sand dunes or flat beach lands along the Oregon Coast or along the Coquille River where one finds exciting river washed roots from the torrential rains we are noted for in Oregon. Driftwood includes roots, branches, stumps, lovely knots which are the last remains of a tree because they are such solid wood. Not to be left undiscovered are embedded knots in river beds. Being under water has preserved them, so all that is necessary for use in designs is a good scrubbing with a brush, soap and water. A collection of such knots is arranged in the "Knotty Story" on page 113.

Driftwood may appear uninteresting until it is combined with plant materials. I have stored wood for a number of years, to one day, find just the right plant material and a purpose to use it. Bold flower forms, bright colors and interesting textures bring it to life.

The new approach to drift or weathered wood is to get it up in the air. Visual weight is lightened when the wood appears to float in space. It can be a sculptural work of art alone or become a fascinating flower arrangement requiring a minimum of plant material.

There are many ways that one can apply mechanics to driftwood. Several pieces of wood may be joined into one unit by drilling holes and inserting metal rods or wooden dowels. One can elevate the wood by drilling the base of the wood and inserting a threaded rod which threads into a heavy metal base for substantial balance. By having a variety of bases and different lengths of rod, one has many opportunities for various designs using different pieces of wood. One must carefully study the character of the wood, which direction it is going before fastening it to a rod or base. Excess branches that hinder the design or hide exciting open spaces should be removed. Height can be achieved by adding lighter branches for gradation.

Depending on the type of drift or weathered wood one decides whether it would be suitable to paint, varnish, use shoe polish or leave it in its natural silver condition. If one wants to emphasize wood grain, varnish is very effective. There are various ways of adding subtle color effects with paint rubbed into the wood, crayon, chalk, etc. Sharp contrasts can result from painting shadowed areas with black paint and lighter areas with white paint.

Mechanical aids to use for arranging with drift or weathered wood include Oasis, orchid tubes, small plastic bottles, chicken or rabbit wire, small needle frogs in cups to hold water and heavy leaded needle frog cups for flowers at the base of the wood.

Bold flower forms are natural with driftwood in creative design. Examples of flowers are; dahlias, lilies, hibiscus, orchids, torch ginger, water lilies, gladiolus, sun flowers, zinnias, marigolds, peonies and dozens of other flowers of bold forms. Dry plant materials work very effectively in drift or weathered wood designs; so do fruits, vegetables and unusual foliages.

Weathered and driftwood has endless variety as an inspiration to the arranger's creative ability and is a challenge to creativity in floral design.

(See color illustrations, pages 86 – 88)

SUGGESTED SCALE OF POINTS FOR DRIFTWOOD & WEATHERED WOOD

Classes eligible for Creativity Award

	Expressive (with title)	Decorative (without title)
Conformance	10	10
Design	25	35
Color	15	15
Distinction	15	20
Creativity — Originality	20	20
Expression	15	
	100	100

Abstract Designs

Abstract is an expression of design in which plant material is utilized as pure line, form, color and texture to create new images.

The designers utilize what they consider the essence of the material to communicate with the viewer. Exact detail is omitted. "Under statement" is executed by selective choice of very few objects projecting bold simplicity to design.

Eclectic Design

Definition of "Eclectic":
The selection and combination of forms and
concepts from different sources and periods.

The definition of eclectic may cover many subjects other than floral design. For example: One could serve an eclectic menu of foods from different countries; an eclectic art exhibit could include artists from different periods of time with different styles in painting.

By implementing the term "eclectic" into floral design, it is possible to give the arranger total freedom to create and express originality as one chooses. It is a transition from geometric to Free-Form design and is in the category of Free-Form design. (1977 Handbook for Flower Shows)

It is possible to combine several design categories into one design without having to conform to any one specific design as long as the principles of design are implemented, that it has beauty and contains plant material. It is possible to combine geometric shapes with free form, rectilinear and curvilinear designs. Sensitive selection of materials and restraint are necessary to avoid confusion. This is an advanced arrangers challenge and not recommended for the novice as it takes experience before one should attempt multiple designs and be able to recognize good design.

If the design is non-objective, the objects within the design may be totally unrelated as long as they are pleasing in line, form, pattern, textures, colors and space units.

We alter plant material in order to create beauty but never to the extent of mutilating the plant material by taking away its natural beauty which is our goal in flower arranging.

It is the designer's choice to create a design governed only by the exhibitor's desire to create a new and beautiful image conforming to the Principles of Design. Eclectic design is an exciting design category giving a wide variety of choices for the arranger to create new and exciting futuristic designs. It is the arranger's "free for all". It can be a collection of several different objects from different places, time, country or a collection of colors, shapes, forms and textures. An eclectic design gives arrangers complete freedom to do as they choose, as long as it conforms to the flower show schedule — and is good design. Otherwise, the sky is the limit. We should encourage more eclectic designs in flower shows.

(See color illustrations, page 105)

SUGGESTED SCALE OF POINTS FOR ECLECTIC DESIGNS

Classes not specifying type of Design,
Color Harmony, Suitability to
Placement or Occasion.

Classes eligible for Creativity Award

	Expressive (with title)	Decorative (without title)
Conformance	10	10
Design	25	35
Color	15	15
Distinction	15	20
Creativity — Originality	20	20
Expression	15	
	100	100

Kinetic Design

Kinetic designs are those in which movement or appearance of movement is dominant.

1. *Mobile* is a grouping of forms whose suspension is in perfect balance. It depends on air currents for actual free movement. It has a kinetic rather than a static nature and is very fluid. It provides a changing series of plane-form-space-color relationships, responding to its environment in unexpected ways.

2. Designs with programmed or motorized movement are also kinetic.

Mobiles

A Mobile is a grouping of freely suspended forms having visual balance. It depends on air currents for actual free movement.

Balance is essentially the most important consideration in making a mobile. Actual balance as well as visual balance is necessary to attain perfect balance of the objects in the mobile. A mobile must appear to float fluidly in space with each object moving freely in unexpected planes caused by air currents. Movement must not be interrupted by objects being placed so close together that they touch one another. Through the choice of lightweight plant materials such as dried Allim seed heads, seaweed, fragile driftwood, Japanese sea fans, unity can be achieved through repetition of form, size, texture and color, creating interesting spaces within the mobile.

The easiest way to construct a mobile is to start with a sturdy but lightweight free-form object from nature such as dried kelp, seaweed, driftwood or branch, rather than a straight material such as bamboo, which is less artistic and a hard slick surface making it difficult to attach fine wire, fishline, or thread for hanging the mobile. Start at the bottom of the mobile adding objects in an artistic design with balance as your guide. The mobile may be expressive, with a title, or it may be decorative — to be enjoyed for pure line, form, color, texture, space and movement, without a title.

Mobiles make an interesting flower show class and they can be enjoyed by everyone in the home from the babe in the crib to the retired person who has time to sit and watch something interesting and beautiful. Mobiles are an interesting challenge to the creative arranger.

If exhibiting mobiles in a standard flower show, the design must always include some fresh and/or dry plant material because plant materials are the flower arrangers art medium.

(See color illustrations, page 106)

Stabiles

A stabile is also classified as a kinetic design but in a different way than a mobile in that it does not actually move, but gives the appearance of movement.

A stabile is a static sculptural form, fixed in position at the base, which implies motion. It may incorporate moving parts, or a mobile.

Basically, as long as the design is fixed to its base and gives the illusion of movement, there are a number of different approaches one can use to create a stabile.

The examples on pages 107 - 109 will illustrate some possibilities.

SUGGESTED SCALE OF POINTS FOR KENETIC DESIGNS

	Expressive (with title)	Decorative (without title)
Movement	20	25
Design	30	35
Color Harmony	15	20
Distinction	15	20
Expression	20	
	100	100

Assemblages

The classification "Assemblages" is a mid-20th Century trend. An assemblage is a creation of great imagination composed of various elements which may or may not be fastened together. It usually includes unrelated three-dimensional objects, taken from the real world and creatively fused into a new identity showing aesthetic unity. An assemblage exhibited in the flower show must include plant material.

The imagination, ingenuity, and technique of the arranger are the most important qualities.

The word Assemblage includes three different types of designs, all of which are called assemblages. In general, an assemblage is an abstract design containing plant material and object(s). These objects and the plant material are creatively related through their form and color into a new identity having aesthetic unity.

The three types of Assemblages are:

1. *Collage* — an abstract design on a wall-hung panel with plant material, with or without other objects attached. A collage may also be staged on an easel. The characteristic that sets it apart from the other types of assemblage is that it is always done in low relief, fastened and/or glued to its background with minimal third dimensional effect.

2. *Assemblage — niche* — is staged within a niche or against a wall with a background. It is an abstract design containing plant material and objects which may or may not be fastened together and usually includes objects which are unrelated. Objects may be fastened to a panel or background and the entire design unit is three dimensional.

3. *Assemblage — Sculpture* — is a free standing sculptural abstract design which may be staged on a pedestal, against a background or without consideration of a background.
Examples of the three types of assemblage are illustrated on the following pages.

An **eclectic free-form** design with wisteria tendrils enclosing free-form spaces, natural growth of scotchbroom, the skeletonized branches of rhododendron indicate a graceful Hogarth line.

PULSATING RHYTHM

An **eclectic** design using straight blades of New Zealand flax for vertical line, a man-made circle of wicker. Dainty bamboo leaves add height and visual relief to the large radiating circle. A large orange dinner plate dahlia is the focal point of the design.

Sea kelp and coral sea fans form the **Vertical Mobile** suspended with freedom of movement. One pink dahlia holds the center of interest. However, mobiles may have several centers of interest.

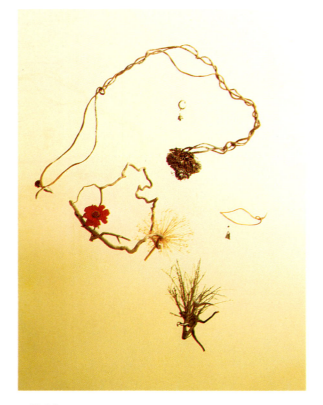

A **Mobile** *suspended from seaweed with an enclosed branch with a red dahlia, suspended skeletonized huckleberry root turning in fluid space.*

"Ebb Tide" — *Another type of stabile with appearance of movement as if floating or drifting with the tide. There are several features of movement in this stabile. The Japanese floats on metal stems give the illusion that they are floating; the sea gull in flight, the pink-white rhododendrons appear as waves and seafoam in movement and in the upper right hand corner is an actual bubble floating — a kinetic accessory.*
The music "Ebb Tide" is very effective to accompany this stabile in a demonstration.

"The Flight" — *is reverse motion of a birds wings dropping from the sky, yet is stationary at the base. The white raised wings are completed with white daisies, carnations and white statice. The design is abstract without complete detail of a bird, just a "statement" of one. Elevated on a thin metal base adds to the airiness of the design.*

"Beauty Hangs By A Thread" — *The forceful branch of Manzanita fastened to its base shows off the floral unit attached to a mobile within the stabile. The negative enclosed space within the mobile adds interest and visual balance to the design.*

"Lift Off" — *Since time began, man has tried to interpret what he sees and how he lives in his time of history. Stone age people carved animals, and whatever they saw, in stone. It is true of our age which is shown in the above stabile. This was the first approach to stabiles in the early 1960's when we were sending the first rockets to the moon.*
The coconut pod, painted a dark green at the base, graduated to lighter color to give thrust. Flowers at the base indicate exhaust of the rocket taking off, orange flowers show ignited power and the nose cone coated with ice as it soars to sub-zero heights.
Note how important the principle, gradation, is to this abstract design.

"Fantastic" — *A rhythmic stabile created from copper tubing
bent in free-form curves and fastened in a lead weighted base.
Coral sea fans covered with colored cellophane add color and
dimension to the design. Fresh plant materials are yellow and
orange tulips, watsonia leaves and varigated hosta leaves. The
design is eight feet tall.*

"Garden Club" — *Is a geometric study of related space areas with interesting texture contrasts and color harmony. Fresh plant material is geranium stems in a styrofoam flower pot cut in half, for a container. Fresh and dry palm leaves add visual weight and interest at the bottom of the collage. Tissue paper painted, velvet gold wall paper and a cork panel are used in making the collage.*

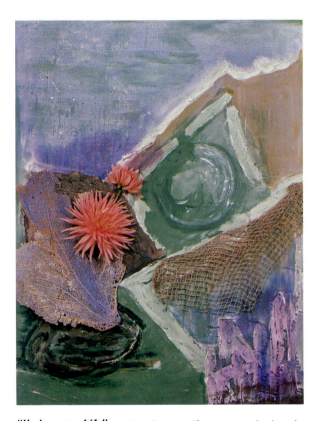

"Underwater Life" — *A collage, as if you were viewing the sea from below the surface. Interesting space areas and texture details are added by acrylic paint on the background. A glass float appears to be lodged among the rocks. A sea coral fan is attached to the collage to which a large pink cactus dahlia and bud are also attached. Vertical coral like plants emerge at the lower right hand corner. Fishnet adds dimension, texture and interest to the collage.*

The rope is the sun for holidays.
    The sea cliff is for adventure.
The crab's claw is sure to get you —
    — if you don't pull the rope fast enough!

May I always live on the Pacific,
    with dahlias blooming at my door.
If you've never been down on the sea cliffs,
    It's time you came west to the shore.

"Sea Cliffs on a Sunny Day" — *Interesting space areas with contrast of shapes, textures and colors, divided by the huge claw which is a separate unit glued one half inch above the surface giving dimension to the collage. Two large orange cactus dahlias are the fresh plant material. The sea cliffs are acrylic paints on a masonite board background. The claw is thin masonite.*

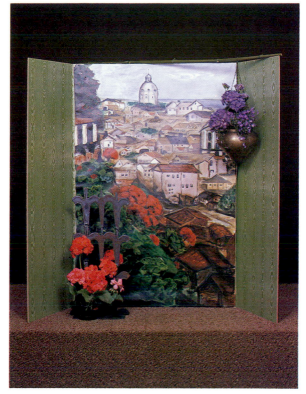

"April in Portugal" — *Inspired by the music of that title, the Portuguese village gives feeling that you are there overlooking the village, on a balmy spring day in the middle of the afternoon. The scent of wisteria wafts past with a gentle breeze as you can hear young children laughing in the distance going home from school.*

The background is painted on a windowshade, incorporating fresh geraniums with the ones painted on the background with a second floral accent of purple flowers in an antique brass container hanging in the design.

UFO — Unidentified Flower Objects" — *Melted green bottles, one suspended by a metal clamp n a rod across the niche, the other stands in a groove in the walnut wood base. A clear panel of 'ass painted with free form design is also suspended and moves freely with slightest air urrents. Flowers are red Cactus Dahlias. Bamboo adds dimension and freshness to the design ithin a niche.*

"Mexico" — *An assemblage within a niche. The background is painted on a window shade depicting a Mexican village with all objects including plant materials, expressive of Mexico.*
Another approach to adding perspective to a design within a niche.

A non-objective assemblage without a title to be viewed for enjoyment of lines, forms, patterns, textures, colors and interesting spaces. Eclectic in spirit, objects are scraps of iron, an old whisk broom, a piece of crude sulfur from a paper mill, green vases were added for contrast in form, color and textures. Orange and red gladiola with red dahlias and Ti leaves complete this study of unrelated but compatible objects.

A non-objective assemblage within a niche emphasizing space, form and color. Plant material is teddy bear sunflowers, in a grouping of green bottles, to carry out the color emphasis in the free standing plate.

"The Knotty Story" — *This is a different approach to a free standing sculptural assemblage. It is a combination of weathered knots found at Bandon, Oregon, embedded in the river and dug out at low tide to be exposed to the weather to attain the lovely silver color. It is not a one unit free standing assemblage but rather several units combined into one design which is a combination of assemblage within a niche and a free standing assemblage. The sculptured knots are staged on a heavy metal base with three heavy rods welded to support them.*

A large piece of burnt driftwood, staged
as if it is weightless is combined with red
dahlias, yucca leaves and a stalk of New
Zealand Flax bloom.

Beauty Remains *The last remains of a weathered tree skeleton has a beautiful silver sculptured form with rich texture features that enhance the accompanying plant materials. The design stands five feet tall and is supported by a heavy metal base and metal rod to which the wood has been wired. Plant materials are large dahlias, bamboo and scotchbroom. The large black circular base visually supports the very large sculptural design.*

"Patricia" — The rhythmic and visual patterns of the song Patricia are carried out in this collage. Black Japanese rice paper has been glued to the artists canvas.
Bright red areas representing abstract flower forms encompass the bright red cactus dahlias which have been inserted through the canvas from the back.
The design is most effective when displayed with the music of Patricia and accompanied with a Spanish dance.

"SS"
A psychedelic design with a contrast of free forms with round psychedelic forms which create motion of inspired images and perceptions that have an aesthetic entrancement and creativity. Easy free flowing rhythm of the white painted birdlike pieces of wood encompass the two psychedelic round forms on the left. Interesting space areas throughout the collage highlighted by one very large cactus dahlia and a Ti leaf.

"Diamonds" — *a rectilinear design of diamond shapes to be viewed for lines, shapes, colors, spaces and shapes rather than forms because they are two dimensional. This is an abstract non-objective construction with a feeling of being architectural and man-made.*

"**Tomorrow**" — is an abstract construction which is eclectic because several choices of geometric forms and shapes from different sources have been combined. It is expressive with title, indicating the mystery, and uncertainty of tomorrow and the indication of celestial expectations in the future.
The design is abstract as it can also be enjoyed for line, space, form, color and texture.

Assemblage

Within a Niche

2.   The assemblage could be made in a niche as several units, created in respect to the space and frame.

The niche is a recessed space or box, designed for displaying the pictorial beauty of the objects in it. It sets the stage in which the several units are displayed.

Interesting space areas are of prime consideration in creating the type two assemblage. This is achieved by contrast of size of the space areas, contrast in form of objects, contrast of bold color, textures with an overall balance displaying several points of interest.

Original painted scenes add interest, mood and depth to the assemblage (April in Portugal - page 111). Lighting can be used in niches as a part of the design technique. The location of the niche light will influence and create moods. Shadows are important since their position and placement may vary. They should be so placed as to create the mood you wish to express.

Depth and interesting shadow spaces can be achieved by placing the light at the side in front of the niche.

Examples of Type II Assemblage follow with explanations of creativity and the arranger's technique in creating them.

Another dimension to the assemblage when for program display, is to add the music to the assemblage.

Things to consider in creating the assemblage within a niche:

1.   Objective — a unite that tells a story with related parts.
2.   Non-objective — unrelated objects which harmonize in texture, color, form and line.
3.   Interesting space relationships.
4.   Color.
5.   Centers of interest.
6.   Lighting effects.
7.   Different approaches to backgrounds within the niche.
8.   Principles, elements and attributes considered in over all design.

(See color illustrations, pages 111 — 112)

Free Standing Sculpture

The free standing sculptor assemblage could be made as one form, a free standing, upright sculptural effect. This type could be staged on a pedestal without consideration of a background. However, the use of a supporting panel of contrasting texture and color, with the addition of special lighting, can enhance the design. The size and form of the panel should be in good proportion and compatible form to the form of the sculptured wood.

Interesting space areas within the free standing sculpture also add interest. Several points of interest should be included in the design without taking away from the sculptural effect. This assemblage suggests natural growth without physical joining. Free form plant materials are used, such as large sculptural pieces of driftwood with the addition of fresh or dry plant materials, and is free form rather than geometric as a construction.

Ways of staging free standing upright sculptural assemblage:

1.   On a pedestal.
2.   Free standing backgrounds to accompany the design.
3.   Introduction of lighting effects.
4.   Color effects.
5.   Size is larger than other design categories.
6.   Introduction of kinetic effects.
7.   Used for exhibition purposes more than for homes.

(See color illustrations, pages 113 — 115)

SUGGESTED SCALE OF POINTS FOR ASSEMBLAGES

Classes eligible for Creativity Award

	Expressive (with title)	Decorative (without title)
Conformance	10	10
Design	25	35
Color	15	15
Distinction	15	20
Creativity — Originality	20	20
Expression	15	
	100	100

Constructions

A Construction though closely related to Assemblage, is generally put together from a limited number of man made objects and has an architectural or geometric feeling and integral use of space. The Construction demands a more selective use of materials, making the ones selected very prominent.

The Construction differs from the three types of assemblages; the collage, units within a niche and the freestanding sculpture in that the Construction is third dimensional not flat like a collage and the entire design is fastened together as one geometric unit.

Constructions can be eclectic in the selection and combination of forms and concepts from different sources and time and can be objective or non-objective with a tendency to be more symmetrical than asymmetrical because of their predominantly geometric forms rather than free forms as in nature. Most man made objects of a preconceived plan are not free flowing.

Constructions have the following characteristics:

1. Bold geometric forms.
2. Intense colors.
3. Simplicity.
4. Pronounced geometric spaces.
5. Abrupt changes in line and forms.
6. Heavy textures — much contrast — coarse or shiny.
7. Entire design unit physically joined — architectural effect.

(See color illustrations, pages 118 — 119)

Psychedelic

Psychedelic designs are forms which create motion of inspired images and perceptions that have aesthetic entrancement and creativity.

(See color illustrations, pages 116 — 117)

SUGGESTED SCALE OF POINTS FOR DESIGN CLASSES

Assemblage — Collage
Assemblage — Within a niche
Assemblage — Free standing sculpture

Classes eligible for Creativity Award	Expressive (with title)	Decorative (without title)
Conformance	10	10
Design	25	35
Color	15	15
Distinction	15	20
Creativity — Originality	20	20
Expression	15	
	100	100

Part 5

ADVANCED ABSTRACT DESIGNS

Rectilinear Design

Rectilinear design is geometric design with emphasis placed on the use of straight lines. The over-all design is not a pre-determined geometric form as found in Conventional arrangements, but is the creative work of the arranger, using much imagination and originality to create an entirely new image.

The form of the overall design gives a geometric feeling. Intricate and various sizes of space divisions are necessary to achieve an interesting design. Rhythm is created by line direction which is repeated and strengthened.

A minimum of round shapes may be used for contrast to avoid monotony but strong emphasis is on the play of straight lines.

Depth in the design is achieved by the overlapping of forms, planes and the gradation of materials. Various techniques in the treatment of plant materials may be used to change original shapes.

As in all Creative and Abstract design, bold color contrasts, strong lines, and interesting textures add dynamic interest to the Rectilinear design. viewed as non-objective for pure line, color and interesting space relationships.

Rectilinear design is exciting and a fresh challenge to the creative arranger who likes to think in Abstract terms. It is an arranger's disciplined game of playing with straight lines.

Characteristics of Rectilinear Design

a. Straight lines must predominate.
b. Over-all form of the design must have a geometric silhouette.
c. Variations of geometric form may be included; triangle, cylinder, cube, cone, sphere.
d. The design must have interesting space variations.
e. Straight lines create a regulated rhythm.
f. Round shapes may be used for accent and contrast but straight lines must predominate.
g. Plant material clipped in moderation to make geometric shapes is permitted but not to the extreme of mutilating the material.
i. Bold color contrasts add interest.

Suggested materials for Rectilinear Design

1. *Fresh plant material:*
   Equisetum, Strelitzia, Heliconia, Cattatil, Aspidistra, bamboo, New Zealand Flax leaves and flower stalk, Gladiola leaves, Yucca leaves, Sansevieria and many others.
2. *Dried plant materials:*
   Wheat, reeds, Cattail, Teasel, Scotch Broom, Pampas Grass, Allium and other straight materials.
3. *Man-made materials:*
   Cork, wire, machinery parts, blocks, dowels, rods, bottles, bricks, hardware cloth, screen, fish net, pipe, styrofoam, copper tubing, stretched fabric, and many "found" items.

Sharp angular geometric enclosed space area of the equisetum gives this design the characteristics of rectilinear design. Emphasis is on all straight lines including the metal stand. Round form is found in the daffodils, leaves and base to break the monotony of all straight lines. But notice how rounded forms are subtly played down compared to sharp angular straight lines.

This rectilinear design was also placed against a white background to emphasize the sharp angular straight lines of the design. The two red Camellias are the only round forms except for the container and base. A palm leaf in radiating lines blends the design unit to the container and gives interesting contrast to the enclosed spaces of the equisetum.

A rather modified form of rectilinear design is found in the skeletonized black huckleberry roots combined with sweet anise and flower heads.
A minimum of round forms are found in the pink Silver Lace Camellia and the seed heads. The design was purposely taken against a white background to show the clear contrast of the rectilinear design. The round container and base give pleasing relief to the otherwise predominantly straight lines.

SUGGESTED SCALE OF POINTS

RECTILINEAR DESIGN	Expressive (with title)	Decorative (without title)
Conformance	10	15
Design	35	40
Color Harmony	20	25
Distinction	15	20
Expression	20	
	100	100

Curvilinear Designs

Curvilinear designs are the direct opposite of Rectilinear designs, with emphasis on rounded forms, irregular contours with a minimum of straight lines. They are very similar to Free Form design with the exception that Free Form design emphasizes the use of organic forms generating from the design, and emphasis on irregular contours. While Curvilinear designs emphasize curved lines, open spaces, and are more abstract. One can use man made objects for form, line, color and texture.

Line is of utmost importance in Curvilinear design as the eye continues along each movement generated in the design, in the same direction even beyond the physical line, until it is re-directed by another stimulus.

If two containers are used, the design is held together by overlapping of lines and planes to support continuance of line through the design.

Rhythm is strengthened when the Curvilinear design develops from a curved or round container and the design is tied together by continuing the lines of the container with the plant materials.

Balance in Curvilinear design, as in all flower arrangement, is perhaps the most important principle. By the use of bold forms with linear material in Curvilinear design, it is more important than ever that physical and visual balance are maintained. Physical balance insures stability. Visual balance is achieved by the placement of the various elements according to size, form, texture, space and color. Dynamic balance indicates movement and freedom through bold use of line which adds strength and interest to the design.

, Curvilinear designs are characteristically open, with space enclosed by rhythmical lines. As in all Creative design, there can be several centers of interest. Plant materials are highlighted when enclosed within the open spaces in the design. Negative space is as important as positive space with careful thought given to simplicity of the over-all design.

Circular movement must not be interrupted by sharp angles and diagonal lines. All Curvilinear design is more pleasing with asymmetrical balance and a gradual flow of rhythm is created by line direction.

Curvilinear designs are more effective if viewed non-objectively for appreciation of pure line, space relationships, forms, colors and textures.

Strong sculptural shapes of materials give the Curvilinear design the bold emphasis combined with vivid colors and sharp texture contrasts which results in a striking silhouette in this Abstract design classification.

Curvilinear Design Characteristics

a. Simplicity is the keynote to a bold design expressing creativity.
b. Graceful rhythm through emphasis of free flowing lines.
c. An open design with rounded enclosed spaces.
d. Conscious use of space, negative spaces are important.
e. Irregular contour, unexpected changes in size of negative spaces.
f. Silhouette dominantly curvilinear, non-geometric.
g. Sharp angles and diagonal lines tend to arrest circular movement.
h. Sculptural organic rounded shapes included in the design, adds interest and breaks monotony.
i. Design may have several centers of interest.

Curvilinear Plant Materials

1. *Fresh plant material:*
   Curved branches, Philodendron, round leaves such as Saxifraga, Aralia, Begonia, Scotch Broom in curved lines, Fatsia.
2. *Dry plant materials:*
   Magnolia, kelp, weathered wood, fasciated mullein, Hydrangea, Palm spathes, Embryo palm, Wisteria, grape vines, corkscrew willow and many others.
3. *Accessories:*
   Sea coral, brain coral, sea fans, round mechanical objects such as disks, wheels, plates, ceramic forms.

Powerful yet graceful lines of smoke tree branch encompass the Allium seed heads in interesting space areas. The organic form at the base of the design is a piece of driftwood and dried fungi. At the base of the stand is the vertebra of a whale which adds roundness to the straight lines of the stand. The organic-shaped container and the round base complete the curvilinear design.

Graceful curves of scotchbroom repeat the oval shape of the pale green container in this curvilinear design. Enclosed space is highlighted with one large orange tulip. Yarrow leaves soften the sharpness of the only straight lines in the curvilinear design. The design could express an Easter theme as the dish placed on a plate holder looks like a huge Easter egg.

SUGGESTED SCALE OF POINTS

CURVILINEAR DESIGN	Expressive (with title)	Decorative (without title)
Conformance	10	15
Design	35	40
Color Harmony	20	25
Distinction	15	20
Expression	20	
	100	100

The Arts Combined

FLOWER ARRANGEMENT
PAINTING
SCULPTURE

Today Flower Arangement has emerged to a place of its own in the world of Art and is recognized as much a part of American culture as painting and sculpture.

Flower arrangement combines the qualities of both painting and sculptor using the same elements and principles but working with a different art medium which is perishable plant material. Floral design has the same three dimensional characteristics as sculpture.

By combining painting and flower arrangement and using sculpture as an accessory if appropriate, exciting new concepts produce new images in the art world today.

"Blue Grotto" — *The background is painted to give the effect that one is inside the grotto looking out to the surf and sand. Special lighting effects carry water reflections and highlight the flower arrangement of white stocks, babybreath and carnations.*

"Garden Fantasy" — *Cinerarias in tints, tones and shades to full chroma are fastened to the back of the artist's canvas and arranged through openings to give the illusion of an abstract garden. Pastel colors and interesting spaces on the canvas add interest and enhance the design.*

"Spring Mist" — A painted panel expressing a misty spring morning, wet with dew and a promise of showers. Accompanying floral units are spring flowers, equisetum and an acient shell embedded rock as an accessory. This is an expressive design.

"The Elements" — A true collage of Japanese rice paper combined with acrylic paint, which represents the elements of the earth of rocks, water, mountains, grass, and sky and it also represents the elements of design in abstract form to be enjoyed for lines, forms, patterns, textures, color and space. It is accompanied by an arrangement of orange gladiolus, red cactus dahlias, yellow marigolds and yellow daisies to carry out the colors in the collage. The heavy black container is the cylinder head of a Volkswagon car.

"FREE AS A DANDELION" —
Tossed by the winds of summer
Over the garden gate
I will attach myself in a garden
No season is too late.

"Indian Summer" — painted by the author as Oregon Coastal mountains look in September and October. The colors in the floral design indicate colors used in an Indian blanket. The container in fall tones and a band of blue which picks up the blue color in the picture. An expressive-decorative combination.

"Oregon Sunset" — *depicting a summer evening on the Oregon Coast just as the sun goes down. The floral design picks up the brilliant colors in the picture. This is a decorative floral design accompanying an expressive picture. The design unit is considered expressive and is not abstract.*

"Tranquility" — *a painted landscape expressing peace and a personal "aloneness" with nature. The design unit is also a double analogous color study. The picture is an analogous color harmony of green through violet. The flower arrangement is an analogous of yellow-green through red-orange.*

"Oriental Reflections" — *has an oriental feeling through the use of plant materials and the indication of a sun reflected from the photographers equipment onto a glass windshield which stands on end in front of the design. The orange and yellow painted panel in back of the design also help carry out the oriental sunset mood. The glass is hardly visible but has great reflection possibilities.*

"Crystal Gem" — *a large glass cube with a dainty floral design enclosed in a crystal container. The transparency design is combining the old with the new. The flower arrangement is a modern replica of the "Tussy-Mussy" which was popular in the late Victorian period when round flower arrangements were displayed under glass domes.*
Glass cube made by Kirk Miller.

"**The Aristocrat**" — *A free-form kinetic design showing free-form of plant growth in the branch and man-made free-form negative spaces in the container. The container is made of 6 inch white plastic pipe and is four feet long. Plant materials are red rhododendron, wild parsnip leaves, manzanita branch and scotchbroom.*

"Suspended Elegance" — *The two copper loops of copper tubing are incorporated into a flexible design. The loops can be collapsed for travel. The inner container, made of giant bamboo, turns from its swivel hanger, independent of the loops which also turn freely. This is a versatile design for home or exhibition.*
Enhanced with tangerine carnations and asparagus fern. It is equally as effective during the holiday season with red carnations and greenery.

"Silver Bows" — *Wide strips of sheet aluminum, attached together at the top and hung by a chain from the ceiling, have free movement with air currents with swivel hooks at the top of each unit. The lightweight aluminum catches air currents which makes the design kinetic. Oasis is attached at the base of the bow to hold water and pin frog for the design. These comprise a unit of three very large designs suitable for a room as large as an auditorium for exhibition. New Zealand Flax leaves wired to wooden picks are inserted into oasis giving a feeling of bows. The design is a mass-line arrangement from the past, introduced into a new design concept. Flowers are units of roses, rhododendrons, pale pink and white peonies and ivy.*

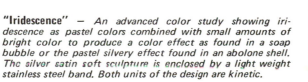

"April Showers" *A conventional mass arrangement of yellow, red and black tulips with babybreath arranged in a yellow ceramic hanging lamp with lighting effect.*

"Chroma-Chromatics" — *Paired free-form containers of heavy, thin steel that has been dipped in chromium. Red and yellow flowers are at fullest chroma, thus completing the title. The designs are kinetic and move independently of each other and have interesting clashing sounds as they touch.*

"Iridescence" — *An advanced color study showing iridescence as pastel colors combined with small amounts of bright color to produce a color effect as found in a soap bubble or the pastel silvery effect found in an abolone shell. The silver satin soft sculpture is enclosed by a light weight stainless steel band. Both units of the design are kinetic.*

"Luster" — is the opposite of iridescency which is a dark background with touches of bright color and white as a reflection such as on a shiny black car or a ripe bing cherry. This design is also a soft sculpture and the opposite side of the iridescency design shown.

"Copper Cut-Outs" — A hanging design of two paired containers with open free-form spaces cut out of the heavy brass water pipe. Open spaces were purposely left free of plant material for interest, contrast and visual weight. Plant materials are orange Oriental poppies, golden chain tree, hosta and fern.

"Space Probe" — *A rocket ship going to the moon. The unusual container was designed for the title and made of sheet metal. It is three dimensional and is kinetic. A new dimension, of sound, is introduced by music created for traveling to the moon with the feeling of speed, fuel injections and thrust as the ship breaks through the sound barrier, then the feeling of weightlessness and malfunctions within the ship. The ship then returns to earth with spiritual and conventional feelings through synthesized music. Special colored lighting effects add excitement to the design.*

"Floral Fantasia" *is a combination of several design categories which includes:*

1. *It is hanging construction.*
2. *It includes a transparency.*
3. *It is a double analogous color harmony.*
4. *A soft sculpture — the yellow-orange.*
5. *It is a kinetic design — both units turn.*
6. *Lighting effect — candle inside black round container.*
7. *Music of "Star Wars" has sound patterns very appropriate to visual forms in the design.*

Fresh plant material of azaleas in yellow to red orange and cinerarias of blue to violet complete the double analogous color study.

"Speak Loudly, Speak Softly" — A Kinetic Vibratile *capable of loud vibrating sounds when struck with metal object, to soft wind chime effects when the hanging design unit gently brushes through the lower metal unit by motion of air currents.*

*New Approaches to
Painting-Floral Design*

1. The picture may be the dominant subject with the floral design playing an insubordinate role through the use of the same colors in lighter value.
2. The picture and floral unit may complement each other in color harmony giving vibrant beauty and interest.
3. A *decorative* unit could include a floral painting with the flower arrangement in color harmony or a close repetition of the painting.
4. An *expressive* design unit could include a landscape or sunset as shown on page 135, "Oregon Sunset" where the arrangement repeats the colors of the sky and the sunset.
5. A non-objective abstract painting of bold forms, colors, lines, textures and spaces could be accompanied by a floral design with line material extending into the picture such as the example of "The Elements" in the abstract collage on page 132 for pure visual enjoyment.
6. The floral arrangement could be the dominant interest because of bright colors, unusual textures or other components such as a sculpture with the accompanying picture painted in subtle greyed tones and absence of details, giving it a soft look with simplicity.

There are many other approaches to combining painting and floral design, it is the challenge of the creative artists to create their own new images. One should avoid equal interest of the two units, to avoid restlessness, confusion and monotony. There may be several points of interest throughout the combined design unit but one should be dominant to hold interest.

The reason that painting-flower arrangement combinations are becoming so popular in America today is because they are adaptable to our culture, in the home, the office, public meeting places such as libraries, churches and many other places where people can enjoy them, as well as at flower shows.

For exhibition programs, music can be introduced as a new dimension to floral design-painting combinations to add expression and life to a new exciting creative trend in American Floral Art today.

(See color illustrations, pages 129 — 136)

SUGGESTED SCALE OF POINTS

Vibratile

Principles of Design	30
Sound & Motion	20
Distinction	10
Creativity — Originality	15
Conformance to Schedule	15
Condition	10
	100

SUGGESTED SCALE OF POINTS

Painting-Flower Arrangement Combination

Classes eligible for Creativity Award	Expressive (with title)	Decorative (without title)
Conformance	10	10
Design	25	35
Color	15	15
Distinction	15	20
Creativity — Originality	20	20
Expression	15	
	100	100

Transparency Designs

Transparency designs are a design on, in, or in back of glass, viewed by light shining through it or by projection of special lighting effects from different angles to create new reflection images. The design should have a "fluid" quality as that found in Mobiles. Depth in the design unit is an important factor to consider.

Transparency designs may include backgrounds; they may be a design surrounded by glass or any other treatment of glass to create new reflection images.

Transparencies may be eclectic in form and spirit with the designer's choice of materials. The only requirements are that the design unit must have fresh and/or dry plant materials arranged according to the principles of design to create beauty, distinction, simplicity and harmony. It may be expressive or purely abstract.

(See color illustrations, page 137)

SUGGESTED SCALE OF POINTS FOR TRANSPARENCY DESIGNS

Classes not specifying type of Design, Color Harmony, Suitability to Placement or Occasion.

Classes eligible for Creativity Award

	Expressive (with title)	Decorative (without title)
Conformance	10	10
Design	25	35
Color	15	15
Distinction	15	20
Creativity — Originality	20	20
Expression	15	
	100	100

Futuristic Designs of Tommorrow

Aerial Designs

Aerial designs are another form of kinetic floral design. Because they are closely related to Mobiles and Stabiles, they are considered an Abstract Design category under Creative Design.

Mobile — is a grouping of freely suspended forms having visual balance depending on air currents for actual free movement in changing planes.

Stabile — is a static sculptural form, fixed in position at the base which implies motion.

Aerial Design — has characteristics of both, a Mobile and a Stabile because it is attached to its base which is at the top and has actual movement as a Mobile but movement is restricted to rotating movement because of being in a fixed position and the design unit is of much heavier, larger forms and is not influenced by air currents. The design may have dual movement within the design, the inner unit rotating independently from an outer enclosure which also turns. An example of this is shown in the design "Suspended Elegance" on page 139.

Aerial designs are to be viewed from all sides, with adequate space around the design so that it does not touch supporting mechanics on either side. The design should appear to float in the air with chain or other means of hanging as inconspicuous as possible.

Aerial designs are the result of the arranger's original concept. It is a design category offering the greatest freedom for creativity since it is not bound by rules, codes, styles or conventional patterns. The design may be kinetic, eclectic, free form, include geometric forms, made of naturalistic materials, man made objects, or can be totally abstract in which plant material and other components are utilized as pure line, form, color and texture. Balance is the most important principle in aerial designs.

Mechanics

In Creative Design where there may be several points of interest, small containers are an important mechanic, used with small needle frogs, wire, tape, orchid flasks. Oasis is very useful in aerial designs especially when working with natural wood, as it fits into irregular areas and is light in weight. Even though aerial designs are heavier than Mobiles, it is best to keep the entire design unit as light as possible for easy rotating movement and convenience of hanging.

Swivel hooks in various sizes depending on the weight of the design, are a necessity in aerial designs to give them freedom of movement. One can purchase swivel hooks at hardware stores and very tiny ones can be purchased at a fishing tackle shop. Mechanics include most of the usual aids to flower arranging plus any new discoveries that fit the purpose without taking away from the distinction of the design. Heavy fishline is ideal for hanging the design as it is practically invisible and will give the design a look of floating in space.

Methods of Hanging

There are several ways of hanging designs other than from a ceiling. One runs into difficulty with ceilings either being too high or of not being permitted to install hooks.

Wood or Metal standards inserted into substantial bases to support the design with a metal rod across the top are very effective and attractive ways to stage hanging designs. The units can be made collapsible for traveling and storing when not in use.

Folding Screens with several panels supporting each other with the designs hung in the open spaces between the folds are another satisfactory way of exhibiting hanging designs.

Wall Brackets if far enough away from the wall and strong enough to support the design are also effective for hanging designs.

(See color illustrations, pages 138 — 144)

CHARACTERISTICS OF AERIAL DESIGNS

1. The design unit should be large and dominant.
2. Bold Forms.
3. Bright colors.
4. Interesting enclosed spaces
5. Absence of detail — emphasis on simplicity
6. Striking contrasts in color, form and textures.
7. Great originality and distinction.
8. Design should appear to float in space.
9. The design unit may include several separate units..

Aerial designs are very adaptable in our homes today as well as arrangement classes for exhibition. They are a refreshing new concept to floral design.

SUGGESTED SCALE OF POINTS FOR AERIAL DESIGNS

	Expressive (with title)	Decorative (without title)
Movement	25	25
Design	25	30
Color Harmony	15	15
Distinction	15	15
Creativity and Expression	20	15
	100	100

Part 6

Point Scoring Comments

DESIGN

ELEMENTS

Line	Form	Pattern	Texture	Color	Space
Continuity	Rounded	Busy	Crisp	Density	Fluid
Angular	Full	Interesting	Delicate	Bright	Exciting
Clean	Dimensional	Pleasing	Compatible	Bi-Color	Irregular
Sharp	Exciting	Confusing	Thick	Cloudy	Monotonous
Interrupted	Different	Inappropriate	Sparkling	Blemished	Inadequate
Confused	Bold	Complex	Exciting	Vibrant	Unusual
Smooth	Beautiful	Airy	Soft	Sunny	Round
Contour	Heavy	Restless	Sharp	Exciting	Free Form
Fluid	Irregular	Formal	Shiny	Cheerful	Related
Brief	Organic	Informal	Dull	Bizarre	Variety
Lively	Geometric		Rough	Conservative	Square
Tension			Satiny	Harsh	Uneven
Strong				Full Chroma	Smooth
Heavy				Thin	Dimensional
				Advancing	
				Receding	

PRINCIPLES

Balance	Dominance	Contrast	Rhythm	Proportion	Scale
Dynamic	Effective	Striking	Restless	Adequate	Large
Equal	Weak	Exciting	Regulated	Too large	Small
Interesting	Inadequate	Pleasing	Monotonous	Too small	Incompatible
Forward	Bold	Monotony	Exciting	Bulky	Life Size
Unequal	Strong	Unrelated	Smooth	Enormous	Comparison
Unstable	Overpowering		Tension	Extravagant	
Complex	Holds attention		Fast		
			Gradual		
			Graceful		

DISTINCTION	CREATIVITY	EXPRESSION	MOVEMENT
Elegant	Ingenuity	Communicates	Free
Superior	Unusual	Conforms	Static
Extra Ordinary	Contrived	Sensitivity	Inhibited
Excellent	Avant Guarde	Relates message	Easy
Fabulous	Bold	Bold	Unexpected
Highest quality	Bright Colors	Brief	Visual
Dazzling	Unusual use of usual	Trite	Physical
Outstanding	Imaginative	Tells story	Exciting
Beautiful	Bold Statement	Objective	Restricted
First Class	Rare choice of components		Non-objective
Extra Ultra	Unexpected effects		
Neat	Unlimited ideas and images		
Flawless			

Aids to Point Scoring Comments

IF THE DESIGN IS SUPERIOR:

Excellent	Design communicates well to observer
Superb	Design is exceptionally good because
Elegant	Good color grouping
Distinctive	Clean silhouette of linear materials
Outstanding	Elegant rich use of textures
Magnificent	Over-all design relates to order
Extraordinary	Simplicity through choice of materials
Distinguished	Excellent gradation
Splendid	Distinction in the highest form

IF THE DESIGN IS GOOD   OR AVERAGE

Adequate amount of fresh materials, dry materials
Pleasant color harmony
Sufficient dominance
Reasonable relationship of materials to title
Comfortable balance
Satisfactory use of textures
Appropriate design for the class
Attractive use of accessories, dishes, or other objects
Use of fresh plant materials reflects good taste
Mechanics neatly hidden
Technique of mechanics is good
Accurate use of color for a color study
Scale is appropriate

IF THE DESIGN IS POOR

Unrelated use of color, texture for title
Design lacks distinction because of poor choice of textures
Conflicting lines
Monotonous space relationships
Title unrelated to class
Use of accessory is unnatural
Insufficient plant material for container
Confusion of line
Ineffective use plant materials
Not bold enough color
Color disharmony
Simplicity is lacking
Design is ill-contrived, too harsh
Balance is ungainly
Balance is disturbing because —
Over-all design is weak because —

Judging Considerations

"Always look for the good in a design as well as its faults. Design is like people — everyone has some good qualities."

The exhibitor expresses an idea within the framework of the schedule; the judge determines how well this has been accomplished.

Following are considerations you might ask yourself when judging a flower show.

SPACE
1. Are the space areas pleasing? Too large, small, monotonous?
2. Do the spaces carry a message of the title?
3. What are they saying to the viewer?
4. Do the spaces affect rhythm? Balance?
5. Are the shapes of the spaces interesting silhouettes, — natural growth linear line, perfectly round, too square?
6. Do the spaces add to the design? Strengthen it?

LINE
1. Are they strong lines that support the design?
2. Do the lines lead to confusion by poor direction?
3. Does the line tell a message of the title?
4. Is rhythm smooth because of how line has been handled?
5. Is there repetition of line throughout the design?
6. Is linear pattern pleasing and exciting? Unusual?

FORM
1. Simplicity achieved by details omitted?
2. Confusion by introducing too many forms?
3. Does the dominant form contribute to the title?
4. Is the dominant form the largest, brightest, most obvious?
5. Is the over-all form of the design three dimensional?
6. Is the form suitable in texture, color, visual weight to the rest of the design?

COLOR
1. Does the color help to communicate the title?
2. What is your reaction to the colors used? Harmonious? Exciting, restless?
3. If it is a color study, do the colors used conform?
4. How does color affect the visual balance?
5. Which color is most dominant, is it in good proportion to rest of design?
6. Is the design good if it were viewed in black and white?

BALANCE
1. What type of balance is used? Is it symmetrical, asymmetrical, dynamic, others?
2. Does the design have good balance, not too forward or backward?
3. How is the visual balance affected by color? Texture, form, placement?
4. What ingenuity has been used to create balance tensions?
5. Is the balance interesting or dull because of placement of materials?

CONFORMITY
1. Does the design conform to class requirements?
2. Is plant material most prominent in the design?
3. How well does the design communicate to the title?
4. Are materials used appropriate for class requirements?

PERSONAL EXPRESSION AND AWARENESS
1. Does the design have a personal statement of originality of the designer?
2. How is sensitivity and awareness expressed?
3. How well does the arranger communicate her idea of the title?
4. Is her originality daring, bold, trite, exciting?

Types of Plant Materials

BOLD FLOWER FORMS	LINE MATERIALS	ROUND FORMS
Amaryllis	Astilbe	Allium
Angels Trumpet	Bamboo	Amaryllis
Anthurium	Beech	Amazon Lily
Artichoke	Bells-of-Ireland	Anemone
Begonia (Tuberous)	Buddleia (Butterfly-bush)	Angels Trumpet
Bird of Paradise	Canna	Anthurium
Black Eyed Susan	Celosia	Artichoke
Blanket Flower	Delphinium	Aster
Camellia	Dogwood	Begonia (Tuberous)
Chrysanthemum	Eucalyptus	Black Eyed Susan
Dahlia	Fire-Thorn	Camellia
Hibiscus	Flowering Branches	Carnation
Hollyhock	Apple-Cherry-Pear-Plum	Chrysanthemum
Hydrangea	Forsythia	Cineraria
Lilies	Foxglove	Coreopsis
Calla	Gladiolus	Cosmos
Canna	Golden Chain Tree	Crocus
Easter	Goldenrod	Daffodil
Rubrum	Holly	Dahlia
Magnolia	Iris	Daisy
Poppy — Oriental	Larkspur	Geranium
Red Hot Poker	Liatris	Gerbera (Transvaal Daisy)
Rhododendron	Lilac	Hibiscus
Poinsettia	Lupine	Hollyhock
Orchids	Magnolia	Hydrangea
Peony	Phlox	Lily
Marigold — (African)	Pussywillow	Magnolia
Rose	Quince — (Japanese)	Marigold
Skunk Cabbage	Snapdragon	Milkweed
Sunflower	Stock	Peony
Tulips	Tritoma (Red Hot Poker)	Poppy
Waterlily	Scotch Broom	Portulaca
Zinnia	Trumpet Vine	Primrose
	Watsonia	Ranunculus
	Wisteria	Rhododendron
		Rose
		Stokesia
		Strawflower
		Succulents — Crassula, etc.
		Tulip
		Water lily
		Yarrow
		Zinnia

FILLER MATERIALS	FOLIAGES
Acacia	Agapanthus
Artemesia (Wormwood)	Aspidistra
Azalea	Anthurium
Bachelor Button	Artichoke
Celosia	Azalea
Basket of Gold	Bamboo
Bleeding Heart	Banana
Blue Lace Flower	Beech
Candytuft	Begonia (Rex)
Clover	Bittersweet
Columbine	Bird of Paradise
Coral Bells	Blue Berry
Dusty Miller (Artemesia)	Caladium
Deutzia	Calla Lily leaves
Everlasting	Camellia
Fern	Cedar
Feverfew	Cotoneaster
Floss Flower	Cypress (Florida)
Forget-me-not	Dieffenbachia — (Dumb Cane)
Fragrant Viburnum	Eucalyptus
Freesia	Euphorbia (Spurge)
Garden Heliotrope	Dusty Miller
Goldenrod	Fern
Heather	Franklinia
Lilac	Geranium
Phlox	Gladiolus leaves
Pieris (Andromeda)	Grapevine
Queen-Anne's-Lace	Holly
Spider Flower (Cleome)	Hydrangea
Spiraea	Ivy
Statice	Juniper
Sweet Pea	Magnolia
Sweet William	Maple
Veronica	Milkweed
	Mountain Laurel
	Rhododendron
	New Zealand Flax
	Philodendron
	Pine
	Salal (lemon leaf)
	Saxifraga leaves
	Scotch Broom
	Watsonia leaves
	Viburnum — Davidi, etc.

Plant Conditioning

NAME	CONDITIONING	WILL LAST
Acacia or Mimosa	Cut branches when ½ in flower ½ in bud. Condition in cold water over night.	1 to 1½ weeks
Adams-Needle (Yucca)	Split stems, condition overnight in shallow cold water.	4 to 7 days
African Violets	Cut with sharp knife, condition over night in warm water.	1 week
Agapantha (Lily of the Nile)	Cut when outer rim of flower cluster is opening. Condition over night in cold water.	7 days
Althea (Rose of Sharon)	Split woody stems, condition in cold water over night.	2 days
Amaryllis (Hippeastrum Reginae) (Lycoris radiata)	Condition overnight in cold water to which 1 tbsp. of ammonia has been added for each 2 qts. water to check bacteria.	4 to 7 days
Amazon or Eucharis Lily	Insert short stems in wet cotton store in refrig. or condition with stems in cold water overnight.	6 days
Anemone or Wind Flower	Cut when petals are wide open but centers tight, or large buds showing color. Place stems loosely in cold water over night.	7 to 12 days
Angels Trumpet (Datura)	Cut in advanced bud stage. Submerge foliage for ½ hour before conditioning stems in cold water.	5 days
Anthurium	Cut when fully open. Split stems, condition overnight in cold water.	1 month
Apple Blossoms	Cut when buds are well developed. Split woody stems and condition in cold water overnight. Can be forced.	1 week
Artemesia or Wormwood	Split woody stems. Condition both flowers and foliage for at least 24 hours in deep cold water.	5 to 10 days
Artichoke (Cynara Scolymus)	Condition overnight in cold water. Drys well, retaining color for dried flowers. Hang up-side-down to dry.	1 month — fresh
Aster, China (Callistephus chinensis)	Cut when ¾ open. 1 tsp. sugar to 1 qt. water. Condition overnight. Revive wilted flowers with stems in 80-100 degree water for short time.	2 weeks
Aster, Hardy, or Michaelmas daisy	Split stems, treat same as China Aster.	6 to 10 days
Astilbe	Cut when panicles are ½ open. Split stems, condition overnight in cold water. Excellent dried for arrangement.	7 days fresh
Aucuba (Aucuba Japonica)	Split stems, condition overnight in first, warm water, then cool.	months - will root in water
Autumn Crocus (Colchicum autumnale)	Cut in advanced bud stage, condition overnight in cold water.	3 to 5 days
Azalea — Rhododendron	Cut when 3-4 florets are open. Split woody stems, condition in cold water overnight. Spray flowers and foliage with fine spray mist.	5 to 10 days

NAME	CONDITIONING	WILL LAST
Bachelors Button or Cornflower	Cut flowers when fully open. Condition overnight in cold water. Tight buds or half-open buds will not open.	5 to 8 days
Balsam or Lady Slipper (Impatients Balsamina)	Cut when ½ flowers are open. Split stems and condition overnight in cold water. Place stems on slant for curves.	5 to 6 days
Babys Breath Gypsophila	Cut when ½ in flower. Condition in cold water overnight. Avoid wetting flower petals. Excellent dried.	1 week fresh
Bamboo (Bambusa)	Submerge in cold water until crisp. Lift leaves but leave stems in water until ready to arrange. Drill holes and fill canes with water to last longer period of time.	1 to 2 weeks
Banana	Submerge in cold same conditioning as for bamboo. Apply lemon juice to cut edge of leaf if trimmed for smaller leaves.	1 week
Barley	Cut after stems are strong enough to support grain heads. Condition overnight in cold water. Excellent dried.	1 to 2 weeks
Basket of Gold	Cut when ½ in flower. Place stems loosely in cold water overnight.	5 days
Beard Tongue (Penstemon)	Cut when ¼ flowering stalk is open. Split stems, condition in cold water overnight.	1 week
Bee-Balm	Cut when ¼ in flower, condition overnight starting with warm water.	5 to 7 days
Begonia (Tuberous)	Cut when flowers fully open. Condition in large container of cold water. Add 1 tbsp. salt to 1 qt. water. Briefly and gently submerge whole flower in clean water, let water drain off. Split stems of flowers and foliage	4 to 7 days
Bells of Ireland	Submerge in cold water 1 to 2 hours. Lift and condition overnight in cold water. Will dry well also.	1 to 2 weeks
Bird of Paradise (Strelitzia)	To each quart of cold water, add 3 heaping tsp. sugar and 2 tbsp white vinegar to obtain PH-4. Cut stems on slant with sharp knife. Remove old flowers and gently lift out new ones.	1 to 2 weeks
Bittersweet	Gather when fruit is brilliant. Spray with clear plastic to prevent shriveling. Fresh, arrange immediately.	Indefinitely
Black Eyed Susan (Rudbeckia)	Cut with sharp knife when blooms are fully open. Condition stems overnight with foliage submerged in cold water.	1 to 2 weeks
Blanket Flower (Gaillardia)	Cut when in full bloom. Add 4 tsp. of sugar to each quart of water. Condition overnight.	7 to 10 days
Bleeding Heart	Cut when ½ flowers open. Split stems condition overnight in cold water.	4 to 6 days
Blue Lace Flower	Condition overnight in cold water almost reaching flower-heads. Place stems on slant for curves.	7 to 10 days
Bougainvillea	Cut when bracts are fully developed and showing color. Submerge stems and flowers in cold water ½ to 1 hour. Lift and keep stems in cold water.	6 to 8 days
Bouvardia	Cut when newly opened flowers. Remove as much foliage as possible. Condition with stems in cold water overnight.	4 to 6 days
Brodiaea	Cut when ½ flower cluster is open. Condition overnight in cold water.	1 to 2 days

NAME	CONDITIONING	WILL LAST
Browallia	Cut when 1-3 flowers are open on stem. Condition overnight in cold water.	4 to 7 days
Butterfly Bush Buddlea	Cut when ½ flower spike is open. Split woody stems. Remove foliage, place stems in hot water 80-100 degrees. If wilting occurs, repeat process. Fine spray helps freshness of flower heads.	5 to 8 days
Cactus	Condition with stems in water overnight. Blooms continue to open.	1 day
Caladium	Split stems, condition overnight in cold water. Submerge leaves completely for ½ hour in cold water if wilting.	5 to 10 days
Camas Lily	Cut when ¼ of flower spike is open. Split stems and condition overnight in cold water.	4 to 8 days
Camellia	Cut when blooms are partly open. Insert stems in a box of wet cotton, spray with fine mist of cold water, cover and store at 45-50 degrees overnight.	3 to 8 days
Candytuft	Cut when flower clusters are ¼ open. Split woody stems, remove foliage, condition overnight starting with warm water. Annual type use cold water.	5 to 7 days
Canterbury Bells (Campanula)	Cut when stalks are ¼ to ½ open. Condition in hot water of 100 degrees to start, let remain overnight.	1 to 2 weeks
Cardinal Flower	Split stems and sear ends in flame for 15 seconds, then place in warm water let remain overnight.	5 to 7 days
Carnations	Condition overnight in cold water up to flower heads. After arranged, spray with fine mist but not enough to drip.	10 days
Cast Iron Plant Aspidistra	Submerge leaves in cold water about one hour then place leaves upright in a few inches of water overnight. Curves or lines can be achieved by rolling or tying leaves and submerging in water.	Months
Castor Bean or Castor Oil Plant	Condition flowers in cold water 1 to 1½ hours. Foliage, split stems and condition in warm water to start with.	10 days
Cat Tail	Gather early in Season — June-July, Spray with clear plastic or dip in clear shellac immediately after cutting to prevent shatter. (Or hairspray).	Indefinitely
Cherry Blossoms	Single bloom, cut when only few buds open. Condition in cold water overnight or warm water to hasten bloom.	5 to 15 days
Chinese Balloon or Bell Flower	Cut when 2-3 flowers on a stem are completely open. Split stems and place in boiling water for 1½-3 minutes or sear with flame to count of 15. Place stems in sugar solution 4 tsp. sugar to 1 quart warm water.	5 to 7 days
Chinese Lantern Plant	Gather when fruits are vivid orange and papery texture. Dry upright. When dry, spray with clear plastic to preserve pods. Green pods, condition stems in cold water overnight.	Dry-indefinitely
Christmas or Lenton Rose	Split stems and condition in deep water overnight.	For weeks
Christmas Trees	Keep tree outdoors as long as possible before decorating. Place trunk in pail of warm water to start. When ready to decorate, place in cool part of room in pail of sand and keep moist.	3 to 4 weeks
Chrysanthemum	Cut stems under water. Condition in cold water with 3-4 level tbsp. sugar to 1 qt. water. If wilt, start in 100 degree water, with same amount of sugar. Splitting stems very important.	1 to 3 weeks

NAME	CONDITIONING	WILL LAST
Cineraria	Condition flower clusters overnight with stems in warm water first. Foliage decays rapidly. Cut flowers before pollen in center is mature.	5 to 7 days
Clarkia	Condition with roots in water overnight or cut stalks with 3-4 florets open. Condition overnight with stems in cold water.	5 to 8 days
Clivia	Cut when ½ cluster is open. Condition stems overnight in deep cold water. Recut stems from florist.	2 to 3 days
Clover	Cut when flowers are ¾ open. Remove foliage, condition overnight in cold water. Also dries well.	5 to 8 days
Cockscomb (Celosia)	Condition overnight in cold water. Remove unnecessary foliage. Place on slant for interesting curves.	1 to 3 weeks
Coleus	Condition overnight in cold water. Will develop roots in water.	2 to 3 weeks
Columbine (Aquilegia)	Cut when 2/3 of flowers open on stem. Condition at 45-50 degrees with stems in cold deep water. Avoid wetting flower petals.	5 to 7 days
Coral Bells	Cut when ½ spray is in flower. Condition overnight with stems in cold water. For curved stems, allow to wilt slightly then place on slant in water	5 to 10 days
Coreopsis	Condition overnight in cold water to flower heads. Add 1 tbsp. salt to 1 qt. water. Condition at room temp.	1 to 2 weeks
Cosmos	Condition overnight in cold water up to flower heads. Cut flowers without pollen and do not cut buds as they will not develop into blooms.	5 to 8 days
Cotton	Treat as woody material. Split stems and condition overnight in deep cold water.	Fresh – 1 week Dry-indefinitely
Crepe Myrtle	Condition stems in warm water. Cut when some buds in cluster begin to show color.	1 week
Crocus, Spring	Cut in advanced bud stage. Condition overnight in cold water.	3 to 5 days
Croton	Wash in cold water, split woody stems, condition in cold water overnight. Roll, tie, submerge in water for interesting line and curves.	3 weeks
Cushion Spurge (Euphorbia)	Cut when cluster is ½ open. Sear stem in flame count slowly to 15 or place at once in hot water 80-100 degrees and let remain overnight.	5 to 8 days
Cyclamen	Pull fully-opened blossoms and leaves from plant, do not cut them. Split flower stems and leaves and condition in cold water overnight.	5 to 8 days
Daffodils or Jonquils (Narcissus)	Kept in 48 degree dark room. Will hold up to 2 weeks. Condition overnight with stems in 3-4 inches cold water.	5 to 8 days
Dahlia	Condition in water as hot as your hands can stand. Leave in dark cool place overnight. Remove excess foliage under water.	5 to 7 days
Daylily (Hemerocallis)	Select stems with a number of buds as each bloom lasts just one day. Condition overnight in cold water.	1 day
Delphinium	Cut when half the florets are open. Condition overnight in cold water. Storage of 48 to 53 degrees best. Place on slant for curves.	5 to 10 days

NAME	CONDITIONING	WILL LAST
Dock or Sorrel	Gather at various stages of development. Excellent fresh or dried.	Indefinitely Fresh 5-10 days
Dogwood	Condition overnight with stems in warm water. Split woody stems.	7 to 10 days
Dracaena	Cut where leaves join plant, taking as much stem as possible. Wash leaves in cold water, split stem, condition overnight in cold water.	2 weeks
Dumb-Cane (Dieffenbachia)	Remove foliage where stem joins plant. Condition overnight in cold water.	2 weeks
Dusty Miller (Artemesia)	Foliage is more useful than the flower. Split stems, condition overnight in hot water 100 degrees to start. May take second such treatment recutting stems.	5 to 10 days
Edging Lobelia	Lift entire plant when half in flower. Wash soil from roots, condition in cold water overnight. Combines well with English Daisies, Pansies etc.	4 to 8 days
Empress Tree	Cut panicles when 3-4 flowers are open. Split woody stems and condition overnight with stems in warm water to start.	3 to 5 days
English Daisy	Cut flowers when ¾ open. Split stems, condition overnight in cold water. Revive by recutting stems and placing in 80 to 100 degree hot water.	7 to 10 days
Eucalyptus	Split stems, condition overnight in cold water. Dries or glycerins well.	2 weeks-fresh Indefinitely Dried
Fern, Asparagus	Plumosus variety, refrigerate with stems out of water, stored at 48-50 degrees. Sprengeri variety, place stems in cold water, condition overnight.	1 to 2 weeks 2 weeks
Fern, Cinnamon	Place fronds in flat container of cold water so completely covered. Remove in 1 hour, drain and stand upright in cold water PH-4, until used. Presses well.	2 to 3 days
Fern, Maidenhair	Submerge cut fronds in cold water 1-2 hours. Keep stems in cold water until used. Presses well.	2 to 3 days
Feverfew	Cut when ½ of florets are open. Condition overnight starting with warm water.	1 week
Firethorn (Pyracantha)	Split woody stems. Condition overnight in warm water to start with.	5 to 7 days
Floss-Flower (Ageratum)	Cut when ½ flowers are open. Condition overnight with stems in warm water.	5 to 7 days
Flowering Tobacco (Nicotiana)	Cut when 1-2 flowers fully open. Condition overnight stems in warm water.	2 to 3 days
Forget-me-not	Condition stems in 80-100 degree water to start. May have to recut stems and repeat process if wilting occurs.	5 days
Forsythia	Cut branches just beginning to bloom. Cut below or through the node. Place in cold water overnight. Forces well.	1 to 3 weeks
Fox Glove	Cut when ¼ to ½ flowering spike open. Condition stems in warm water overnight.	5 to 10 days
Frangipani	Cut when flowers ½ open. Sear stems in flame for 15 seconds, then condition stems overnight in cold water.	1 to 2 days

NAME	CONDITIONING	WILL LAST
Franklinia	Condition overnight in cold water. Split woody stems.	2 to 4 days
Freesia	Cut when 2-3 flowers are well opened. Condition overnight with stems in cold water almost up to flower heads. Store at 45-50 degrees until used if possible.	2 to 3 days
Fuchsia	Split woody stems, hold stems in boiling water for 1½ to 3 minutes, then place in cold water overnight. Fine mist is also beneficial.	5 to 7 days
Garden Heliotrope (Valeriana Officinalis)	Condition overnight with stems in warm water to start with. Very fragrant.	6 to 10 days
Gardenia or Cape-Jasmine	Split woody stems, condition overnight in cold water. Spray both flowers and foliage with fine mist of cold water. Place short stemmed flowers on wet cotton and store at 45-50 degrees.	4 to 6 days
Geranium	Cut clusters when ½ in bloom. Split stems, condition in cold water overnight. Condition hairy types by first placing in warm water 80-100 degrees, then in cold water. (Rose Geranium).	5 to 8 days
Gerbera, Transvaal Daisey	Cut when fully open. Avoid touching centers. Cold water to flower heads.	5 to 7 days
Geum	Condition stems in warm water first and remain overnight. Tight buds will not open in water.	5 to 7 days
Gladiolus	Cut when second floret is ready to open. Cut about 2 p.m. when flowers are slightly wilted, this delays opening of buds. Recut stems and condition in cold water overnight.	3 to 5 days Florets last 1 to 2 days
Globe Thistle	Cut when ¼ of the globe is covered with open flowers. Split stems, condition in cold water overnight.	1 week
Glory Lily (Gloriosa)	Cut when flowers are fully open. Split stems, condition in cold water overnight.	4 to 5 days
Golden Chain Tree (Laburnum)	Cut clusters when ½ open. Split stems and condition overnight starting with warm water.	1 to 3 days
Golden Marguerite	Cut stems with a few fully opened flowers. Condition overnight with stems in cold water. Will develop curves if placed on slant during conditioning.	7 to 10 days
Golden Rain Tree (Koelreuteria)	Cut when flower clusters are ½ open. Condition overnight starting with warm water.	3 to 4 days
Goldenrod	Condition stems in cold water overnight. Dries well.	1 to 3 weeks
Heather	If flower tips wilt, condition in warm water 80-100 degrees. Dries well.	1 to 3 weeks
Hibiscus	Split stems and condition in cold water for at least 4 hours. Cut the same day you plan to use them.	1 to 2 days
Holly	Submerge branches in water to remove residue. Keep berried holly in water in cool dark place. Do not use metal container.	For weeks
Hollyhock	Split stems 5-6 inches, sear ends in a flame counting slowly to 15. Condition stems with warm water to start with.	5 to 9 days
Honeysuckle	Split stems and condition overnight in cold water.	4 to 7 days
Hyacinth, Dutch or Grape	Use sharp knife, split stems and place in cold water overnight. If they wilt prematurely, dip stems in boiling water for 1-3 minutes, then in cold water. Wrap with wax paper to hold fragrance.	4 to 6 days

NAME	CONDITIONING	WILL LAST
Hydrangea	Split stems about 1 inch. Remove extra foliage. Hold stems in 2-3 inches of boiling vinegar and count to 30 slowly. Condition overnight in deep cold water adjusted to pH-4.	4 to 9 days
Iris — German, Japanese or Siberian	Cut when first bud is ready to unfold. Condition overnight in cold water. Avoid sudden temperature changes.	3 to 5 days
Ixia	Cut when 2-3 florets are fully open. Condition overnight with stems in cold water.	2 to 3 days
Jacobinia	Split woody stems and remove leaves. Place stems in warm water overnight.	5 days
Jerusalem Cherry	Remove unnecessary foliage, split stem, condition overnight in cold water.	5 days
Kerrybush (Kerria japonica)	Cut stems to the ground, split woody stems, condition overnight in cold water.	5 days
Lantana	Split stems, condition in hot water 80-100 degrees. May have to repeat conditioning.	6 days
Lavender	Cut when spike is half in bloom. Split stems, condition overnight in warm water to start with.	10 days
Lemon-Verbena	Cut when flowers ¼-½ open. Split woody stems, condition overnight in hot water 80-100 degrees to start. Spray flowers and foliage with fine mist of cold water. Defoliating will retain freshness.	7 days
Leopards-Bane (Doronicum)	Cut when flower petals are turned back but centers still tight. Condition overnight in cold water almost up to flower heads. Place slantwise for curve.	12 days
Lilac	Cut when ¼ to ½ open. Remove all foliage. Split woody stems at base. Pull away outer bark for 3-4 inches. Place in cold water overnight. Spray with fine mist of cold water.	3 to 5 days
Lily — Calla	Condition with stems in cold water for only 4 hours. Submerge stems and leaves in cold water for 1 to 2 hours.	1 week
Lily — Canna	Cut when first 2 florets open. Split stems and condition overnight in cold water.	2 to 3 days
Lily — Easter	Cut when 2-3 flowers in each cluster are open. Split stems and condition in cold water overnight.	5 to 8 days
Lily — Rubrum	Cut after petals turn back and recut stems under water. Split and condition overnight with stems in cold water.	5 to 8 days
Lily of the Valley	Cut when ¼ spray is open. Condition overnight in cold water.	3 to 7 days
Lupine	Cut when flowering spike is half open. Remove most foliage. Condition over night with split stems in cold water. Stems curve to light, and when slanted.	7 days
Magnolia	Split woody stems, scrape bark away from base. Condition overnight in cold water.	4 days
Maltese Cross	4 tsp. sugar to each qt. of warm water. Cut when less than half the flowers in each cluster are open.	Up to 7 days
Maple	Condition overnight with stems in warm water to which 2 to 4 tsp. sugar has been added for each quart.	1 to 2 weeks
Marguerite, Boston or Paris Daisy	Recut stems under cold water, condition in same water overnight or longer.	6 to 12 days

NAME	CONDITIONING	WILL LAST
Marigold	Cut when centers are tight and petals reflexed. Recut stems under cold water before conditioning overnight. Zinc sulphate will retard decay. 1 tsp. to 1 quart of water.	1 to 2 weeks
May-Apple	Remove leaves to expose flowers. Split stems and condition in cold water overnight.	3 to 5 days
Mexican Sunflower	Cut when flowers are fully open. Cut buds for interest. Condition overnight in warm water to start with.	5 to 9 days
Mignonette	Cut when flowers are ¼ way open or less than ½ the spike is open. Condition in 80-100 degree hot water then cool water overnight.	5 to 7 days
Milkweed	Cut when half open. Sear stems for 15 seconds to prevent wilting.	4 to 6 days
Mistletoe	Wrap in wax paper and keep refrigerated until ready to use. Otherwise split stems and place in cold water overnight. Does not keep well in warm room.	2 weeks
Mockorange	Remove ¾ of foliage, condition overnight in warm water.	5 to 10 days
Monkshood	Cut when 1/3 spike is in flower. Split stems and condition in cold water.	5 to 7 days
Mountain Bluet	Cut just before flowers are opened. Split stems and condition in warm water overnight. Petals are very fragile.	4 to 7 days
Mountain Laurel	Cut when half in flower. Condition overnight in warm water to start with.	3 to 5 days
Dusty Miller	Cut when 2-3 flowers open on each stem. Recut before conditioning overnight in warm water. (Stems dry quickly).	4 to 6 days
Nasturtium	Gather fully opened flowers and large buds. Break stems away from main stem. Recut, split stems, condition overnight in cold water.	3 to 5 days Leaves last 1 to 2 weeks
Oleander	Cut clusters when half in flower. Split stems, sear in flame, count slowly to 15. Remove excess foliage. Condition overnight in warm water to start with.	7 days
Orange Blossoms	Cut when 1/3 to 1/2 flowers open. Split woody stems. Condition overnight in warm water to start with. Submerge non-flowering branches in cold water 1 hour.	3 to 6 days
Orchids	Depending on the variety some last longer than others. Blooms take 3-4 days to open fully. Place in 48 degree temperature away from drafts. Wrap in wax paper in refrigerator and put in covered box to keep moist.	Up to 20 days
Painted Tongue (Salpiglossis)	Condition overnight in cold water up to flower heads.	4 to 7 days
Pansy	Pull blooms rather than cut from plants, with as much stem and foliage as you can. Condition overnight with stems in cold water. Lasts longer if you lift whole plant.	4 to 6 days
Passion Flower	Cut well developed buds with petals showing color in late afternoon. Or cut fully open flowers just before arranging, condition 2-4 hours in cold water.	1 day
Pear	Cut when only ¼ of branch is in flower or will shatter. Split woody stems, condition in cold water overnight or until blooms are open. Can force anytime after Christmas.	5 to 15 days

NAME	CONDITIONING	WILL LAST
Peony	Cut when blooms are less than ½ open. Split stems. Place in cold water.	7 to 9 days
Periwinkle (Vinca)	Buds continue to open. Cut when 2-3 flowers are open on each stem. Split stems, condition overnight in cold water. Remove upper foliage to show off flowers.	3 to 5 days
Peruvian Daffodil and Tiger Flower	Recut stems under water after removing fully opened flowers from plants. Condition 1 to 2 hours.	1 day
Peruvian Lily	Cut when ½ buds are open in clusters. Split stems, condition overnight in cold water up to flower heads.	4 to 5 days
Petunia	Cut when fully open. Condition overnight in cold water. Add 4 tsp. sugar to each quart of water. Remove excess foliage below water level.	4 to 7 days
Philodendron	Cut stems below node. Condition in cold water overnight.	1 month or more will root in water
Phlox	Cut when clusters are ½ open, condition overnight in cold water.	7 to 12 days
Pieris (Andromeda)	Cut when clusters are half open. Split woody stems, condition overnight in cold water. Submerge new growth for one hour to avoid wilting.	8 to 10 days
Pitcher-Plant	Submerge flowers and foliage about ½ hour until firm and crisp. Split stems, condition overnight in cold water.	7 to 10 days
Plum	Cut when ¼ open. Split woody stems, condition overnight in cold water. Easily forced for spring bloom.	8 to 10 days
Poinsettia	Immediately after cutting, put stems in boiling water for 2-3 minutes or sear stems in flame counting slowly to 15. Condition overnight in cold water.	4 to 5 days
Poppy — California	Condition overnight with stems or roots in cold water. Buds will close at night but will open again next day.	4 to 6 days
Poppy — Oriental	Cut in advanced bud stage. Sear stem ends immediately counting to 15. Sear stems at length to be used in final design. Then condition in deep cold water overnight or at least 8 hours.	4 to 5 days
Portulaca	Lift whole plants if possible to place in low container. Condition overnight with stems or roots in cold water.	3 to 6 days
Primrose	Cut when cluster are ½ open. Split and condition overnight in warm water to start. May have to repeat process if wilt occurs.	5 to 8 days
Pussywillow	Cut when buds begin to swell or cut when ¼ to ½ of branch is in bloom. Split stems and condition in cold water. Also keeps well out of water.	5 days fresh Indefinitely (dry)
Queen Annes Lace	Cut at any stage. Condition overnight in cold water reaching almost to flower heads. Avoid wetting flowers. Also dries or presses well.	7 to 12 days
Quince — Flowering	Cut when ¼ or less buds are open. Split woody stems and condition in cold water overnight. Buds continue to open indoors.	2 weeks
Ranunculus	Cut when ¾ open. Split stems, condition overnight in cold water up to flower heads. Stems will curve if placed on slant in container.	6 to 12 days

NAME	CONDITIONING	WILL LAST
Redbud	Cut budded branches before flowers open. Split woody stems, put stems in hot water 80-100 degrees. Spray daily with fine cold mist to prevent bud drop.	4 to 5 days
Red Hot Poker or Torch Lily	Cut when 1/4 to 1/3 spike is open. Split stems, condition overnight with stems in cold water. Place on slant for curves, or bend with warm hands.	1 week
Rhododendron	Cut when ½ or less florets open in a cluster. Submerge flowers and stems in cold water ½-2 hours. Split stems and condition in cold water overnight.	7 to 10 days
Rose	Cut stems diagonally about ¼" above leaf. Cut in late hours of daylight. Remove foliage from base of stem. Split stems, condition overnight with stems in cold water reaching almost to flower heads.	3 to 5 days
Rose Mallow	Cut in advanced bud stage. Leave in cold water until buds open.	1 to 2 days
Rosemary	Avoid very young growth. Split stems. Condition in cold water overnight. Revive at 80-100 degrees hot water.	2 weeks
Salvia — Blue	Cut when lower half of flowering spike has opened. Condition overnight in warm water to start with. Stems will curve when placed on slant.	5 to 10 days
Saint Johnswort	Let blooms open fully before cutting. Split stems. Condition overnight in cold water.	3 to 5 days
Satin Flower — Godetia	Lift whole plant, wash soil from roots, trim away excess foliage and buds. Condition overnight with roots in cold water. Larger variety split stems etc.	2 to 5 days
Scabiosa — Pincushion Flower	Cut when almost fully open. Split stems, condition overnight with stems in cold water almost reaching flower heads.	4 to 8 days
Scotch Broom	Cut branches of desired length, submerge in water to freshen and clean. Split woody stems, condition in cold water until used. Excellent linear material, can be shaped for curves etc.	2 to 3 weeks
Sea Lavender	Cut when clusters are half in flower. Condition overnight with stems in cold water. Excellent dried.	5 to 10 days
Sea Pink or Thrift	Cut when flower heads are half open. Condition with stems in cold water overnight.	5 to 7 days
Sedum	Cut when clusters are ½ in flower. Condition overnight with stems in cold water.	7 to 10 days
Shadbush	Cut when not more than half flowers are open on branch. Split woody stems. Condition in cold water overnight.	5 to 7 days
Skunk Cabbage	Cut when flower trumpets are formed, and leaves size desired. Remove stamens and submerge blooms in ice water for 1 hour to remove odor. Keep stems in cold water until used.	8 to 12 days
Slipperwort — or Calceolaria	Cut when half in bloom. Split stems, condition in warm water to start with. Avoid wetting flower petals.	3 to 5 days
Snake Plant or Sansevieria	Flowers are insignificant for cutting. Foliage excellent for arranging in or out of water.	Leaves 4-6 weeks
Snapdragon or Antirrhinum	Cut when half in flower. Condition overnight or at least 8 hours. Water should be pH4 — 3 tsp. sugar to 2 tbsp. white distilled vinegar. Place in hot water 80 to 100 degrees and leave overnight. Curving stems achieved by placing on slant. Will also curve to light.	5 to 12 days

NAME	CONDITIONING	WILL LAST
Snow on the Mountain	Check flow of milky juice in stems with boiling water treatment or by searing in a flame.	Foliage 1 wk.
Spider Flower (Cleome)	Cut when clusters are half in flower. Split stems, condition overnight in warm water to start.	3 to 5 days
Spirea	Cut when ¼ to ½ branch in bloom. Split woody stems. Condition overnight starting with warm water.	4 to 10 days
Spurge — Flowering (Euphorbia)	Cut clusters when half in flower. Recut and split stems just before putting in 80-100 degree water to check milky juice. Let stems remain in water overnight.	1 week
Statice	Condition a few hours in cold water. Cut when fully open for fresh or dried use.	
Stephanotis	Split stems and sear in flame 15 seconds. Place in cold water overnight. Wrap in cellophane or thin wax paper to capture delicate fragrance. Remove excess leaves.	4 to 6 days
Stocks	Cut flower spike when ¼ to ½ open. Split woody stems for 3-4 inches. Condition overnight with stems in very cold water. Spray with fine mist. Add 3 tsp. sugar, 2 tbsp. vinegar to water.	5 to 12 days
Sumac	Cut flowers when panicles are ½ open. Condition overnight with stems in cold water. Remove excess foliage.	5 to 8 days
Sunflower	Cut when petals turn back but tight centers. Split stems condition in 80-100 degree water to start with.	6 to 10 days
Sweet Alyssum	Lift small plants when half in flower or cut individual stems when half in bloom. Condition overnight in cool water.	5 to 8 days
Sweet Pea	Break off slender stems on annual type. Cut Perennial type. Place in warm water with tsp. sugar to 1 qt of water.	5 to 8 days
Sweet Rocket	Cut when ¼ to ½ open, condition overnight with stems in warm water.	5 to 9 days
Sweet William	Cut when half in flower. Split stems and condition in cold water overnight.	1 to 2 weeks
Trumpet Vine	Pick when 1-3 flowers are open. Split woody stems, condition overnight with stems in cold water. Submerge foliage in cold water until firm, about ½ hour.	3 to 4 days
Tuberose	Cut spikes when ½ open. Split stems, place in cold water almost reaching flower heads.	7 to 12 days
Tulips	Cut in advanced bud stage. Condition by wrapping a dozen or so together in wet newspaper in tall container to keep stems straight in cold water up to almost flower heads.	5 to 8 days
Verbena	Cut when 2 or 3 rows of buds are open, showing color. Split stems ½ inch. Condition overnight in warm water, add 1 tsp. of sugar to 1 quart of water.	5 to 7 days
Violets	Pick when fully opened. Submerge blooms in large container of cold water for 1 hour. Remove, shake off excess water, place stems in cold water overnight.	4 to 7 days
Wallflower	Cut when slightly less than ½ open. Split stems, condition overnight with warm water to start with.	6 to 12 days
Waterlily	As you cut each flower, immediately plunge stem into water to prevent air bubbles in the stem. Recut stems and leave in same water about 3 hours.	1 to 4 days

NAME	CONDITIONING	WILL LAST
Wisteria	Cut in advanced bud stage. Split woody stems and condition in cold water over night. Add 3 tsp. sugar to 2 tbsp. white distilled vinegar to bring to pH4. Spray with fine cool mist.	4 to 7 days
Yorktown Onion	Cut when one half open. Recut stems before placing in cold water to condition overnight. Place on slant for curving stems.	4 to 7 days
Zinnia	Cut when completely open but centers tight. Remove lower leaves. Plunge in cold water to condition overnight as soon as possible after cutting.	1 to 2 weeks

Glossary

ABSTRACT DESIGN: A creative art form, in which plant material and other components are used solely as line, form, color and texture, with space, to create new images.

ACCENT: Emphasis, importance.

ACCESSORY: Anything in an arrangement in addition to plant material, container, base, background or mechanics, subordinate in the design.

ACHROMATIC COLORS: Colors lacking hue and chroma; neutral colors — black, white and gray.

ADVANCING COLORS: Red and those colors in which red predominates as well as other warm hues.

AESTHETIC DESIGN: Design having attributes of harmony, beauty, distinction and expression.

AMATEUR: One who cultivates any art for the love or enjoyment instead of professionally for gain.

ANALOGOUS COLOR SCHEME: Generally, no less than three adjacent hues, no more than one-third of the color circle and no more than one primary using closely related colors.

ARRANGEMENT: Fresh cut plant material organized in a container or on a base.

ARTIFICIAL: Not natural; made or manufactured to simulate natural appearance.

ASSEMBLAGE: A creative art form. An arrangement of plant material, or objects and plant materials, which may or may not be fastened together. Objects are related through form, color, and/or texture, but need not be related functionally or emotionally. Objects must be natural size.

ASYMMETRICAL BALANCE: Nearly equal visual weight composed of different elements on each side of a vertical axis. Balance without symmetry.

BACKGROUND: May include back, sides and surface beneath an arrangement. It is the surface against which an arrangement is viewed.

BALANCE: A design principle, visual stability.

BASE: An optional component used in the design under the container or under plant material such as mats, natural woods, or stands.

BEAUTY: A design attribute. That intangible quality which evokes aesthetic pleasure and delight.

CHROMA: The strength or weakness of a hue, the purity of color, a dimension of color.

CHROMATIC COLORS: All colors other than neutral colors. Colors with the presence of hue and chroma.

CHROMATIC DESIGN: The color design.

CLASSICAL STYLE: Characterized by simplicity and restraint; a style of Japanese flower arrangement.

COLLAGE: An abstract design of plant material, with or without other objects, fastened to a wall panel, organized in low relief.

COLOR: A design element. The visual response of the eye to reflected light rays.

COLOR WHEEL OR CHART: A color circle expanded to include values by addition of varying amounts of black and white.

COLOR CIRCLE: A circle with hues in the same order as they appear in the solar spectrum.

COLOR DIMENSIONS: Hue, Value and Chroma.

COLOR HARMONY: Color schemes organized according to the principles of design.

COLOR TRIANGLE: A triangular chart showing color from pure hue through tint to white, tone to gray, and shade to black.

COMPLEMENTARY COLOR SCHEME: Colors directly opposite on the color wheel.

COMPONENTS: Plant material, container, background and mechanics of a flower arrangement.

CONDITION: The physical state of plant material or horticulture specimens at the time of judging.

CONTAINER: Any receptacle for plant material or other arranging components.

CONTEMPORARY: Belonging to the same period of time.

CONTRAST: A design principle. The use of opposite or unlike elements, qualities or forces.

CONTRASTING COLOR SCHEME: Hues, values and/or chromas farthest apart.

CONVENTIONAL STYLE: According to guides, rules, or frequently used design patterns.

COOL COLORS: Based on primary color of blue and colors in which blue has been added.

CREATIVITY: An original concept in the choice of components or in the organization of the design elements within the limitations of the design principles.

DECORATIVE DESIGN: Organization of the design elements to adorn a specific place.

DESIGN: The organization of the design elements in an arrangement.

DESIGN ATTRIBUTES: Beauty, Harmony, Distinction and Expression.

DESIGN ELEMENTS: Space, line form, pattern, texture and color and size. The basic visual qualities of a design.

DESIGN PRINCIPLES: Balance, Dominance, Contrast, Rhythm, Proportion and Scale. Basic art standards based on natural laws.

DISTINCTION: Marked superiority in all respects.

DOMINANCE: The stronger effect of one or more of the elements in the design. Dominance implies presence of subordination.

DRIED PLANT MATERIAL: Plant material from which the moisture has been removed.

DYNAMIC BALANCE: Equilibrium between the force of rhythm and the force of gravity.

ECLECTIC: The selection and combination of forms and concepts from different sources and periods.

ELEMENT: (See Design Elements).

EMPHASIS: Special force, stress or importance.

EXHIBIT: A unit in a competitive or non-competitive class; May also be educational or decorative.

EXHIBITION TABLE: One in which design is not related to function.

FEATURE: Anything in an arrangement in addition to plant material, container, base, mechanics or background, dominant in a design. Or to give prominence to.

FLOWER ARRANGING: The art of organizing the design elements of plant material and other components according to design principles to obtain beauty, harmony, distinction and expression.

FORM: A design element.

FORMAL: Conventional and regular, marked by strict observance of social customs and etiquette.

FRAME OF REFERENCE: The board determined by the surrounding objects.

FREE FORM DESIGN: A creative art form, free from conventional ideas and patterns, within the limits of the principles of design.

FREE STANDING: A design to be viewed from all sides.

FRESH PLANT MATERIAL: Any part severed from a living plant in fresh condition.

FUNCTIONAL: Pertaining to implied practical use or purpose.

FUNCTIONAL TABLES: Those which are designed for the service of food.

GRADATION: A sequence in which there is regular and orderly change. It may be in size, form, color or texture.

HARMONY: A consistent, orderly, or pleasing arrangement of parts.

HOGARTH CURVE: An arrangment following the line of a lazy S named "the line of beauty" by Hogarth.

HUE: The name of an individual spectrum color such as yellow, red, green.

INFORMAL: Without ceremony; casual.

INTENSITY: (See chroma).

INTERMEDIATE HUES: Hues between the primary and secondary hues bearing the name of both hues as yellow-green; blue violet.

INTERPRETIVE DESIGN: Selection and organization of the design elements to suggest a theme, idea, occasion, mood or atmosphere.

KINETIC: Pertaining to motion. Motorized or by air currents.

LINE: A continuous visual path. A design element.

LINEAR: Made of or pertaining to line.

LINEAR FORM: A form in which length is the dominant dimension.

MECHANICS: Contrivances used to hold and control materials in design.

MINIMUM: A very small amount.

MINIATURE: An arrangement five inches or less in every dimension. All design principles apply with scale being most important.

MOBILE: A grouping of suspended forms having visual balance in which actual movement can be induced by air currents.

MONOCHROMATIC COLOR SCHEME: Variations in value and/or chroma of a single hue.

MOTIF: Outstanding feature or theme in a design.

NATURALISTIC: Representing an actual scene or using plant material as it grows.

NCSGC: The National Council of State Garden Clubs, Inc.

NEUTRAL COLORS: White, black, gray; completely lacking in chroma and hue.

NICHE: A recessed space.

NOVICE: One who enters competition for the first time or who has won no awards in previous Standard Flower Shows.

OP ART: The use of aggressive forms of equal strength, equal hue, and equal luminosity that demands visual perception.

ORIGINALITY: The product of one's thought and imagination. May apply to choice of materials or to the manner of usage.

PATTERN: The silhouette created by a combination of lines, forms, colors and the spaces between them. A design element.

PERIOD STYLE: That of a designated historical era, including the present.

PLAQUE: A conventional design of plant material, attached to a wall hung panel, done in low relief.

POINT-SCORING: The evaluation or grading of exhibits using a scale of points for the particular design being judged.

PORCELAIN: Translucent ceramic ware.

POTTERY: Glazed or unglazed earthenware.

PRIMARY COLORS: The pigment primaries are red, yellow and blue; and are the colors from which, theoretically, all other colors are derived.

PRINCIPLE HUES: Primaries of red, blue and yellow; secondaries of orange, violet and green.

PRINCIPLES OF DESIGN: Basic art standards used to organize design elements. These principles are balance, proportion, scale, rhythm, dominance and contrast.

PROPORTION: The relationship of the length, area, or volume of one part to another or of one part to the whole. A design principle.

PSYCHEDELIC DESIGN: Forms which create motion of inspired images and perceptions that have aesthetic entrancement and creativity.

PURE COLOR: Hues in which no white or black is present.

RADIATION: Lines extending out from one central axis — as plant material extending out from focal point.

RECEDING COLORS: Blue and those colors in which blue predominates.

REPETITION: The repeating of size, form, color, direction in a design.

RHYTHM: A dominant visual path through the design. A design principle.

SATURATION: Same as Chroma.

SCALE: The size relationship of the component parts of a design. A design principle.

SCALE OF POINTS: The value or importance of one category compared to another, expressed in percentages.

SECONDARY COLORS: Orange, violet and green produced when equal parts of two primaries are mixed.

SHADE: A mixture of pure hue and black; a dark value of a hue, as opposed to a tint.

SHADOW BOX: A lighted recessed space, the front of which is covered with translucent material. The light within the box is placed so that the shadow of the enclosed objects make a silhouette on the covering.

SHAPE: A form predominantly two-dimensional.

SILHOUETTE: The outline of an arrangement against its background.

SIZE: The dimension of a line, shape, form or space.

SMALL ARRANGEMENT: Not to exceed eight inches in any dimension.

SPACE: The open areas in and around the arrangement. The three dimensional expanse within which an arrangement is organized. A design element.

SPECTRUM: A series of color images formed by the refraction and reflection of the sun's rays in concentric bands of color as the rainbow.

SPIKE: A lengthened flower cluster in which the flowers are practically stemless. Example Gladiolus, delphinium.

STABILE: A static sculptural form, fixed in position at the base, which implies motion. It may incorporate moving parts or a mobile.

STILL LIFE: A traditional art form. An arrangement of objects and plant material in which the objects are featured and the theme, if any, is interpreted more by the objects than the plant material. The objects have a relationship based on use or emotion, or are things often seen together. They must be natural size.

STIMULATING COLORS: Colors that attract the eye involuntarily: bright hues with high visibility, strong chromas.

STYLE: A characteristic manner of arranging.

SUBORDINATION: Subduing or making less emphatic or less important; implies the presence of dominance.

SYMMETRICAL BALANCE: Similar on two sides of a real or imaginary vertical axis.

SYMMETRY: Regular repetition of like or similar elements on either side of a median line, plane, or central point.

TEXTURE: The quality of the surface structure, such as rough, smooth, dull, shiny, etc. A design element.

TINT: A mixture of pure hue and white. A light value as opposed to a shade.

TONE: A hue that has been grayed by adding black.

TRADITIONAL: Handed down from the past.

TRANSITION: Plant material chosen to give gradation between the center of interest to the tapered outline of a design.

TREATED PLANT MATERIAL: Plant material whose appearances has been altered, but is still recognizable as plant material. This includes glycerinizing, painting, or alteration by any method. Minimum amount permitted in Standard Flower Show only when specified in the schedule.

TUSSY-MUSSY: A concentric circle of small flowers arranged around a large central flower.

UNITY: The relation of all parts; a harmonious whole; oneness.

VALUE: The lightness or darkness of a color.

VASE: Container for displaying specimen.

VOLUMETRIC: Three-dimensional space.

WARM HUES: Red and those hues in which red predominates.

WEATHERED WOOD: Weather-worn, seasoned or affected in form, color and texture by exposure to the elements.

Index